Also by Tom Pow

In the Becoming

New and Selected Poems

TOM POW

Polygon

First published in Great Britain in 2009 by Polygon,
an imprint of Birlinn Ltd
West Newington House
10 Newington Road
Edinburgh
EH9 1QS
www.birlinn.co.uk

ISBN: 978-1-84697-122-8

British Library Cataloguing-in-Publication Data
A catalogue record for this book is available on request from the British Library.

Typeset by Koinonia, Manchester
Printed and bound by Athenaeum Press Ltd., Gateshead, Tyne & Wear

for Julie, Cameron and Jenny

Contents

from *Landscapes and Legacies* (2003)

from *Sparks!* (2005)

from *Transfusion* (2007)

from *Dear Alice: Narratives of Madness* (2008)

New Poems

Acknowledgements

The poems collected here are drawn from the following collections: *Rough Seas* (Canongate, 1987); *The Moth Trap* (Canongate, 1990); *Red Letter Day* (Bloodaxe, 1996); *Landscapes and Legacies* (iynx, 2003); *Sparks!* (Mariscat Press, 2005); *Transfusion* (Shoestring Press, 2007) and *Dear Alice: Narratives of Madness* (Salt Publishing, 2008). I am grateful to the publishers of these volumes and to the editors in whose magazines many of the poems first appeared.

Of the new poems, 'St Andrews' was written for *The Book of St Andrews* (ed. Robert Crawford, Polygon, 2005). 'St Nicholas' is a revised version of a poem that first appeared in *There's a Poem to be Made – in celebration of Stewart Conn's 70th birthday* (ed. Christine de Luca and Ian McDonough, Shore Poets, 2006). Poems in this section have been previously published in *Markings*, *New Writing Scotland* and the Scottish Poetry Library *Poetry Reader*.

Many thanks to Lilias Fraser for her enthusiasm for the initial idea of a *New and Selected*. Thereafter, I am grateful to Stewart Conn for encouraging me to view it as a book which should have its own organic life – subject to 'an undertow of the poet's own priorities, a satisfying of inner longings and compulsions'. My in-house editor, Sarah Ream, has been exemplary in her understanding of such issues. Her attention to detail and her view of the bigger picture have led both to tighter punctuation and to a judicious reordering of a number of the poems to reflect the changed dynamic that selection brings.

I have had cause to be grateful to many people – family, friends and fellow-travellers – for support, succour and encouragement while writing the poems that appear in this book. Some of them are named in the individual collections; others, I hope, will know who they are. My gratitude again to all. But my biggest debt is to my wife, Julie. The generosity of her spirit – 'a mystery and a blessing' – has safe-guarded time and space without which many of these poems wouldn't have been written.

Not a single annunciation,
a flashing sweep of celestial power,
but the imprint of a voice, as it praises

what in each moment is prefigured –
by the smell of wild garlic,
by a broken blue shell.

from *Rough Seas*
(1987)

Invitation

Step through
the ragged hawthorn
into the park:
by a frozen pond
a muffled toddler
has absconded.
See her make
a clockwork run
at a scattering fan
of silver birds –
her open arms raised
in a gesture
of hopeless desire.

Early Years

Each New year, over a glass of sweet sherry,
she told the story of how they met.
She was sixteen and had travelled from Wick
with a friend. In a flurry
of snow he picked her up from the remote
station and took her to the farm
where she was taught
to cook flapjacks, befriend Indians, shoot
straight at grizzlies and stifle the blushes brought
on by the free curses of the ranch-hand
who sat in her basin of dough.

Mostly though, they'd lived in Edinburgh,
where George grew roses and worked for the GPO.
But they kept the bloom of those early years
well-watered: their two daughters lived them through
till their own ghostly youth was shelved.
Then, alone, each night she kissed his photograph
and, at New Year, giggled as she told
how that man had exploded: 'Dough!
Thank God. I thought I'd ruptured myself.'

Half Day

I

We lay in a hammock of grass and heather
below the broken neck of Arthur Seat:
the city around us like a lake of quartz,
yet here so still, so far from the buses
trawling Princes Street, we could hear crickets
clicking in the grass. We netted them
like minnows from gently bowing stems;
coffined their green, quivering bodies
in a matchbox. Mother – impossibly young –
turned her face to the sun and we basked
in her ease and indifference: uniforms
rucked beneath us; nodules of heather gathered
on woollen socks. 'Look, children, over there.'
Her voice drifted down to us, airy as lace.
Even we hadn't noticed till it was
centre-stage: a childlike cumulus
over the ruined ark on Calton Hill.
Our eyes blinked in the brightness, the strangeness
of moving from our miniaturised world,
where heather stems were gnarled trees and crickets
roaring dragons, to this huge conjuring trick.
We had grown with the frail calligraphy
of aeroplanes, the rockets' scarlet bloom;
but there was magic in how this stayed afloat
and in a world which wanted it. More so,
when Mother told how they'd even made the war
convivial – whole streets out to watch
as two droned over the shuttered city,
harmlessly released their bombs and chuntered off.
And this too looked so plumply good-natured,
you could never imagine it doing wrong,
allied as it was to the beneficent world
of circuses, balloons and giant combs.

We cast our darker selves in the heather
and stood up in the dizzying sun. If only
the power of our thoughts could hold it there,
or else a generous white fin scoop us home
(via the green Lothians, the shimmering Forth),
we would be saved from the workaday world
with its huffy queues and stuffy buses,
and Mother's mouth stiffening in tiredness
on the final hill; the afternoon frittered . . .

II

All the dandelion clocks in the waste ground
had been blown to blind button-eyes, when we flicked
away spent grasshoppers, tight as beech-buds,
and joined the others in play. Our summer energy
was white-hot – we turned afternoon into
yesterday, easy as an old coat –
but the litmus of memory burned slower
and that night something passed over me in sleep;
high up, like the Leviathan that spreads
its ancient rafters over the City
Museum's cold Gothic spaces, its flesh
hanging from it in tattered banners.

Holiday Down South

One afternoon, draped in cast-offs,
we performed a plotless masque
beneath the laden plum tree.

At interval, we poured lemonade from a jug
that needed two hands. Laughing, they tipped it
beneath their deck chairs.

They preferred the cider my uncle served
from a fat barrel by his shoulder.
They preferred their wartime stories.

Later, an aeroplane droned by the moon
and all my aunt's chintzy roses
were blotches of blood.

Rising from her nest of blankets, my sister
called me *Silly*. 'One 'plane doesn't make
a war,' my aunt smiled.

And so they thought to have calmed me.

'Ever seen such plums?' my uncle asked.
Those last ones were the colour of old blood:
the slightest pressure split them.

Words

The oar creaked in its sprocket
like a rotten tooth – yet we were carried
across the Almond, from city to country
as if by magic.

Hand in hand along Dalmeny shore, I thought –
how beautiful she is, and told her so.
Laughing uneasily, she gave me
the top of her head to kiss.

I was one of a line of blessed men –
men with Continental Leanings: down the ages
the Levelling sunlight had fallen on all
our uncollared, unbuttoned, white shirts.

'I don't want to get married,' I said –
conjuring the words from the faint sea breeze,
my heart beating faster with excitement
and surprise.

And again – later or earlier – alone
in Princes Street, on the clearest East coast day,
I ran my eye round the city's towers

and I said to myself, 'City, lovely city,
I must leave you.' And the words flew from me,
free as pigeons I never thought or cared
would come to roost.

The Master of Vailima

'Home no more home to me, whither must I wander'
                      Robert Louis Stevenson

The Master of Vailima leans on the high
      veranda. He is posterity's dandy; a rickle

of shins, shrouded in white, black-belted
      as a buccaneer. Behind him the shadows

of airy, redwood rooms and the green mount of Vaea
      rising. Here, surely, a spirit could breathe –

far from the haar and coasts bristling
      with patriarchal achievement. Illness it was

sealed the child in him – implacable Blind Pew,
      like a claw around his wrist, leading him

to the darkened room, where archipelagos of leaves
      were mapped out in sunlight and Cummy's voice

rolled out, like the sea. And illness it was
      which, at last set him free

to a more wholesome escape than piss-ups
      at Rutherford's and the *frisson*

of childhood whores. Free, he became
      the world's eye: a bright lens turning

over the dark and distant oceans, making 'of his mind
      a map', where the restless traveller

need never stop. Even at Vailima – the prayers
      for his Gothic tribe of dependants; kneeling

over the indifferent earth – was there ever
      an arrival? Was this desperate encampment

home? The trade winds, like an insistent
      amanuensis, script over the watery graves:

'There are other kinds of scaffolding, Father;
      lives to make, as well as save.'

The River

1. Evening Sketch

Night squats on the grey estate: the river,
the roads turn black. Up a deserted side-street
darkness tears away from a nakedly
lit shop-front: Mini-Cabs For Hire. Inside
a man, slumped on a frayed red settee, snores
before the TV's vertiginous greens.
C & W, here is your soul: in this glimpsed
interior or on the waterfront,
where the hamburger man stares idly
through his caravan's tight lozenge of light,
as two drunks, leaning into each command,
duel over their mongrel's affections.
Later, in a bright, packed snug, one will lie
amongst broken glasses, weeping her shame,
as *he* casts narrow glances round the bar –
blue eyes blazing with fright and challenge.

2. Flight

Someone kicks the blown pod of a mixer
to life, triggers a flock of birds. They rise
from their clenched roosts in a dark fan: splinters,
filings – a taut hawser, suddenly snapped,
disintegrated, sucked beyond a grey
Zeppelin of cloud to where riverside
chestnuts shadow the milky amnion
and we appear – we, the giddy ones – corks
on the earth's black waters. We are learning
slowly about pain: that however deeply
we trawl it, we will bob up again
into this cool, indifferent morning.
Here, to pluck the last overblown roses:
to watch birds fall on the lawn, like ashes.

3. Flood

Rather the sour dampness of her own rooms
than a Home. Rather the sofa's chaos –
the urinous news, the anti-diet –
than the more orthodox regime.
Here to await Death, like one of Cavafy's
Senators, vast camiknickers soaking
up the blasting gas fire. Only a flood
could move her and, when the waters do rise,
two policemen arrive. Her neighbours stand
at the edge of the great creeping puddle,
when, in the beam of a torch, she edges
her zimmer forward. Her hand trembles briefly
on her shawl – a gift meant for Christmas –
but her light-trapped face shakes off its tears.

4. Night Walk

In the evening park, swings hang preter-
naturally still: horseshoes of packed ice
catch the pale moonlight. Deep in his enclosure,
the fallow deer tucks his nose into his haunches
till he is perfect form – stone or mask:
though the dark seaweed of his horns crowns him
like an ancient curse. Through black conifers
the cream turret of the local museum
commands the town: its death mask is a prize
amongst the rusting leg-irons. And what
has this chalk edifice to tell – the thin lips,
the fin of the nose – of evil? The moon
sidles from a cloud, looks down on the blank
physiognomy of this night, this park, this town.

5. Summer Ritual

On hot days, the boys left their riverside
camp fire beneath the viaduct to swim
and clown about in the centre of town.
Desperate beings! The sun ran down
their knuckled spines; dried the wet scallops
their buttocks left on the wall in lines. Soon
a challenge grew: who could walk the white seam
of the weir, cupping water in his hands?
We waved at countless waxen soles, watched
armless bodies totter and twist, to see
who could seal their sparkling gift and bear it
across the water. In the end, one was dredged
from a feculent pool; his pale face veined
by a lime-green weed, his fingers dripping tears.

6. The River by Night

It's strange to hear that clear bell toll over
the containers' nocturnal manoeuvres:
it reminds of *pensions* in foreign towns
with the shutters open wide and, as here,
lights strung out along a river. The waterfront
ruffles like old flesh, each eddy drawing
a meniscus of light, an infinite
tremor of energy. In such domains
I read the capacious remedies of love,
the twisted spools of memory, which burn
but don't go out. Yet this night river soothes
something deeper still, I can no more name
or touch than foretell where tomorrow's gulls
will land – or try the hunger of their beaks.

The Ship

Once proud barques moved up the river,
bringing wine and spices from Bordeaux.
The small ports carried currencies
fat with foreign vowels: *ducadouns*,
Spanish *reals*, Old English groats.

There's still profit in their situation:
a fine view over the river's curve
of a small white sail tacking upstream,
the kinetics of oyster catchers,
their beaks flaming in the sunset.

Most years though bring only more silt
and haafnetters shaking their heads at
so much silver for the whisky's gold
and the poor salmon catch. Where once
ploumdames, liquorice, the finest

French linen were sold, the Hotel
directs its Sunday drinkers as a
car park overflow. While bored children,
fearing their clipped futures may lie
in the mysterious apathy

of the bus shelter (those silent
coupling bikes), use ragged pot-holes
as a stone-horde, a reservoir of splash.
Then one year, like a queen honouring
a lost colony, a French bulk carrier

docked. Its picture in the paper
took up two pages; a grey mass
suckling the small white-washed village.
Families drove from the nearby town
to picnic in its lee, for France

had never seemed so far away, nor all
they stood in, owned and ate, testament
to the ancient dignity of trade.
And yet from its shadows, I felt
a darker world tugging at me

with the strangest undertow; saw
caps rain down as a liner slid
into a grainy sea and banks
of lives, which had all been lived, wave
wildly from every gleaming rail.

It was like finding one's future
somewhere in the past: a fine silt
which worked its way into each crack
of all the plates which float our lives,
causing each one, in turn, to fall

like petals from the hull. Gasping,
I clung to the crude raft of work;
in darkness, cleaved to a body's
warmth; turned small-talk to rivets
before dreading the depths of sleep.

Then one night, after a few drinks,
three of us left the rooted crowd,
picked our way through the black brooding
graveyard of overnight containers –
and boarded. The insistent throb

of disco was a sounding-board
for silence – insectlike, complete –
as we felt our way to the prow
like smugglers. There we took command.
The river brought us the faint tang

of the sea and endless shots of night
within which we lost the landscape's

bearings. Mountain, forest, hillsides –
all dissolved in darkness. Lights
sparkled here and there along the river's edge –

the friendly lights of settlements
where succour would be given to each
who had a need. So this – this
was Nile, Amazon, Limpopo . . .
Linking arms, we made a pact

to dissolve what we'd become, to hold
onto this profligate world
of dreams and possibilities,
as the dull clang of living history
sounded hard beneath our feet.

Witches

*Sources: three photographs of collaborators taken by Robert Capa in Chartres in
August 1944; voices from witch trials, Dumfries 1650s.*

I

Brought to the Prefecture de Police,
*she must confesse her sin and scandall
and be rebuikit* with the rest. Already the courtyard
is littered with their shaved pelts.

Capa takes them, in their shame, standing alone
against the crumbling brick wall, either side of a sturdy
wicker chair – a parody of bourgeois domesticity –
this trinity of mother, daughter and new-born child
a terrible foulness has marked.

The story goes, *He did command
that she fall down and worship him
and if she wold not worship him that she wold worship
his staff and if she wold not worship him or his staff
that she wold worship the Divell.*

But now none can tell whether Death's Head,
fear or sheer sadness moulded the passivity
in her still-young face, dulled the averted eyes
till the blind softness at the bald nape of her neck
is as eloquent about her fate. (Note though the dimple
set in her chin: the Devil indeed is dissembling.)

Her mother's dark-shadowed head is flanked by Buddha's ears,
but – in her powerful fifties – she peers at us
through severe owl-like glasses more as a teacher
whose children disappoint. Only the open mouth
betrays horror. That and the right hand which grasps
a fistful of her long black dress, holding onto temper
or dignity, while her left grips an empty feeding bottle,
a ghostly ring of milk at its bottom.

With these two hands she cradles the power
which comports her daughter, fills that vessel
with the impulse to mother. Thus, the heavy arms which fold
round the swaddled child, which support the thumb-
sucking, dark-haired head, are a vague
tribute from mother to mother.

II

In carnival atmosphere, they are swept
through the cobbled streets of Chartres
under the perfect eye of the cathedral. She holds her baby
close, stares into its face for the only innocence.
The gendarme escorting them smiles like a traffic cop:
this crowd is mostly women and fearless girls
at their heels in floral summer frocks.

They callit her base jade howre and ane witch
and they laugh in her face: one young woman
addressing us with such abandoned beauty
it seems her love chimes with the camera.

And should she not laugh on a warm August day
when the flags of Liberation barely ruffle, when the fear-
mongers become the afraid? Laugh, for at this moment at least,
all evil, the worst possible luck has landed
with another and she been called to book?

III

Now Capa leaves them to return
to their ever-changing house; to close shutters,
to live in shadows, to turn mirrors to the wall.
A million pleasures will become strangers to them –
arranging flowers, finding comedy in fault, breaking bread
with neighbours.

Instead they will sit in silence, bonded by blood and despair –
till their door is chapped
till the first stone is thrown
till they hear 'German Bastard' in every idle shout.

Hair will not sooth them
nor the crying child. Between the three of them,
how can the water of love ever flow freely?

Still, the world will not weaken.
By such tiny crimes, the Great Horrors
are constituted. 'God help us,' cried Elizabeth Maxwell,
tried by Thomas Crauffurd, the Prodder –
'We have meslet skins, we sit neir the fyer.'

A Favourite Stretch of Disused Railway

Dalbeattie to Dumfries line

I

Turn sharp right off the forestry track.

You're on a path of large granite chips
shrouded by silver birch. This will lead you
onto the viaduct. Here the birch become
glossy saplings, the stones one long rockery
for wild strawberry, for the palest green shoots.

From here you can see how well-appointed
the big houses are; their stables boarded up now
and windows broken, but your eye led to them
by the fold of the landscape, by the command
of trees, as surely as in any Claude.

A hawk skims the variegated tops
of an arboretum – cypress, copper beech,
improbable monkey puzzle. Your spirit
goes with it – for you are halfway
to flying here, riding these great arcs of air
with only a mane of rough red stone to hold onto.

II

At the end of the viaduct, a broken grey stile.
The path weeps into a green baize, stitched
with tiny white stars. A moped, clogged with rust,
stands alone; the garish flowers on its petrol tank
almost fading as you look. Playful ghosts
crowd in on you. Old beech trees
spread their arms in perfect planes.

III

When the path becomes a path again,
it is a sodden mud-track, a fine silt
of rootless earth, whose depth you could not judge,
if not aware of that broken vertebrae beneath.
One pool, clear of the choking tagliatelle of algae,
still shows the sharp edges of a few pinkish pieces
of granite. Everywhere else, marsh marigolds
sway imperiously on teased-out stems.

IV

This vegetable world delivers you
into a dark valley of blasted rock, where the ghosts
of a hundred dead wills feel exotic. The purest water
drips down a dank face to be caught on the tip
of each asterisk of moss and become – up close –
a reredos of opalescent drops. Green railings
of nettles crowd the base of this achievement:
sycamore, birch, ash stubbornly cling.

V

As I see it, passing through this gorge,
when the carriage was cast into shadow, a passenger –
one bull-necked, ruddy-complexioned, studying
the market price of lambs – sighed dust and smoke
up spidery nostrils, laid his paper on his lap
and glanced up at the blur of rock, so that

when it was past, his blinking eyes just caught
the sun hitting the heraldic bank of wild rose
and giant daisy. And, as the perfect landscape
opened out before him, he heard the auctioneer's
breathless chanting become the sound
of a speeding train.

The Great Outdoors

Eagerly, I climbed after you to a coign
where the broom was unreal – a curdling
of the richest yolks. Beyond it, fishermen
scrambled over rough black rocks

to the sea's swollen edge. Cumuliform
stencils of sand stretched out
across the bay. Suddenly a sound,
as of silence crumbling, caused me

to glance up from the pink campion
I was cupping in my palm to catch you
poised over that part of the path
where granite snuggled into a dyke.

A white signpost read FOOTPATH one way,
FOOTPATH another and, in the bright sun,
I could not tell whether you regarded me
playfully or mockingly and I wondered

which of these arrows you would follow:
your knapsack between your shoulder blades;
the rationed butter seeping
through the tiny combs of bread.

Summer Running

The chestnut that all winter
cast broken rods on the water
now dips a head, full as a bison's,
to drink.

The once bald arterial oak
crowns the field like a green
rococo keep.

And our quiddity? Our glory?

We arrive – new-born –
beneath the green light of birch arrows,
hoping, if we run hard enough,
to live in a season, where the tang of wild garlic
is the only hint of loss

and the haze of bluebells is everywhere,
like desire.

Rough Seas: Three Postcards

I

You can just make out our hotel about
to be wiped out by a mountainous wave.
A nice fiction perhaps, but in fact today
the sea is calm as glass and already
Sally is spread-eagled with the rest,
impressing the sand with her tan. Not me.
I feel more the pull of rough seas – great plumes
of spume rearing over an empty prom:
a winter image on cheap card that yet
can wolf down the summer souvenir wrack.
Once, as children, didn't we thrill to anything,
racing the gentle tide? Now we only

like the sun to touch us; though rough seas call
us to their edge, drench us with simplicity.

II

You can just make out our hotel about
to be wiped out by a mountainous wave.
Not so: just a swell and constant drizzle
keeps us all locked in a seaside cliché.
I've taken to walking alone along
the wet-black promenade, drunk on salt-air,
till, cold as a bobbing gull, I seek refuge
next to a leering postcard stand. I wrap
my stinging hands round a clear plastic cup
and stare out with all other eyes. I find
Sally's love comes at me now like a huge
toppling wave, careless of whatever I am.
At this grey edge, churlishly, I wish
for one who wanted me less, but loved the more.

III

Waves slam the promenade and explode
past the crenellated facades; as much
creature and fire as water, they hang
like a taunt over the routed sea-front.
Driven indoors, we drain each bulletin:
eight brave men needlessly 'Lost at Sea'.
We are shown the beast licking round the rocks
where their craft was broken; the ragged skelfs
that must be last contact for all whose pride
the greedy lens can't touch. I read 'The Wreck . . .',
let the language break over me, but all
seems rhetoric to the plain salty truth –
that for some people Rough Seas can never be
metaphorical: nor words enshrine their pain.

The Rondanini Pietà

We learn from a letter of Daniele de Volterra
to the nephew of the Master, Leonardo Buonarroti,
that six days before his death
he worked all day on this statue.

It is the revised version of what was begun
seven years earlier, when he was already eighty-two.
Of that, the legs of Christ and a severed right arm
remain. The slack legs, the smooth thighs, begin

a gentle, upward-flowing movement ending
in the diagonal alignment of the heads of Mary,
who supports him – and Christ. As in the Pietà
in St Peter's, the pose is impossible, but there

similarity ends. Fifty years have passed.
Fifty years have taken care of his concern
for virtuosity, for rendering the softness
of a face, the fluid cascades of a dress.

And what we have instead is the image
of something that suffers and is true. Figures
that are almost shadows: hatched
with imperfection, slender, infirm;

their barely-featured faces staring
into an endless pit of sorrow. And what we have
is that throwback right arm: polished, strong;
standing by the pair of them like something

lopped from a body, so the body might be free.
'I saw Michelangelo at work,' writes the traveller,
Blaise de Vigenère. 'He had passed his sixtieth year
and although he was not very strong

yet in a quarter of an hour he caused more splinters
to fall from a block of marble

than three young masons in three or four times
as long. No one can believe it

who has not seen it with his own eyes.
And he attacked the work with such energy
and fire that I thought it would fly into pieces.'
Even accounting for increase in age then

it's a mystery why he did not hack off
that bodiless right arm and be done: but left it
almost as if he meant us to contemplate how far
he had travelled from the interests of his youth.

Catterline

for Joan Eardley

A broken bannister of cottages – a track
plunging to a bay like a scallop
whose grassy headlands today
shimmer like Seurats.

Here, in Number One,
the cancer at her back – breakfast
poked through the window – to the end
her life bled into her art.

Four of five of the works they found later
stuffed into holes for the rain –
'Ah Joan,' they say softly,
who knew her then: 'She had nothing.'

But – to her – if there was light enough,
that light was all. On the wildest days,
her easel cairned down, her canvas
took the brunt of the storm

for as long as time would allow.
So that now,
even if you see Catterline
on a day more fitting to Cap Ferrat

than the grey North Sea, still
through the sunshine you can feel
dark elemental rhythms,
white breakers crashing in.

Longing

Inishere, Aran Islands

Were we there
on that basking island
the still loch at its centre
where the blue heron stood
unruffled at our dancing?

Were we there
splintering the calm water
a shoal of silver mackerel
clapping tails in unison
at such a salty kiss?

Were we there? I wonder
now I am here
where lonely peewits call: ●
beyond this poem,
the White Island warrior –
my shield holding my longing in.

Absent Lover

Each morning I lie awake,
conjuring your body beside me;
laying my head on the still brown
small of your back, kissing
a pale, warm buttock.

But at night
we leave the strictures
of time and place to float off,
like Chagall's couple over the still town;
like Kokoschka's to love in the midst
of a passionate universe.

A Taxi of My Choice

Twin Towers, 1983

We are riding up Riverside
in a yellow taxi of my choice;
a beast so powerful, we roll
together and part as it hits
each wave of traffic. The noise
of the suspension at each jolt

so harsh, we feign wide-eyed fear,
yet your commentary runs on . . .
When I see a drunken man push
another to the wall and clear
in the street-light they kiss, then
disappear into the shadows,

you tell me *Cruising* was shot here –
an area of black warehouse walls
and discrete neon signs. And black
too is the Hudson as it sheers

away from light, seeming to fall
into silence like a soft ballad.

And speaking of which, over there
is Hoboken, where ol' Blue Eyes
came from: finest fixer of place
for those who must move on. I share
his feel for this city, the rise
of the wall of lit, shattered glass

to our right – each splinter a life.
An hour ago, above it all –
'The closest some of us will get
to heaven,' the brochure says – love
took a back seat, as we ogled
what creativity and greed

could do. 'That bar of light is Fifth.
That's Brooklyn' – piecing together
the city for me, like some vast
incandescent jigsaw: a gift
to the soul no less than St Peter's
or Chartres. So that now, when I cast

around for some kind of statement
of what *we* collaboratively
can do, I think of that county
of light and hear your accent:
'Down from the blur of New Jersey,
see the Statue of Liberty.'

Riverside. Hoboken. Brooklyn.
Each name is a memory
within which our love can hide.
Like glitter, I have scattered them
from high. There is a part of me
in each yellow taxi you ride.

Love at the (Bronx) Zoo

We walk the icy paths
past frozen ponds, snowed-in enclosures,
where reeds like drifting porcupines
and black huts are all that show.

In the dim warmth of an animal house,
we linger by a tank
with a sandy-coloured,
soft-shelled turtle, the size
of my spread hand. From the long spoon
of its head, nostrils stick out
like tiny binoculars. Eyes,
two silvery stains. When it rises
from the dark green weed, its fins,
like sycamore seeds, brush the window
we peer through. So close is it
and so angled, we see

the thin loop of its down-turned mouth;
almost fancy it would speak.

Back in the Bronx, we don't know
which blind-eyed alley to turn down;
eventually are wrong anyway. We ride around –
a fly caught in deadly nightshade – trying
to reclaim the rim of the highway

past burned-out buildings, waste-ground;
a brazier licking the chill
off some winos.

A battered blue Cadillac jerks
to a stop in front of us. Rusted panels
shake; red tail lights glare
from corroded fins. We sit tight
as the black man's black curses plume
into the winter air. We turn to each other:

sudden neophytes, who might – sleepless, speechless,
in the dark cage of night – hold their soft bodies
close; fear
for love's survival.

The Feast

Fresh Maine lobster
was laid before us – a knuckly scarlet
bouquet; the garlic butter put beside
in a dainty white cruet.

We had been told
how to proceed: first tugging the oblong head
from the fan-tail (a cosy ritual –
the breaking of bread)

before we cracked the brittle armour apart.
Now we could pick at the pink spread flesh,
dipping each flake in the butter
till we reached the grey mess

of brain. At first we glanced
at each other, checking our lobster etiquette,
but, as we warmed to the task,
our appetites set

their own rules. We cracked off legs,
ripped ligaments, sucked slow on salty, hairy limbs
in our own ways; till – best of all – the claws.
It was almost whim

that I looked up then
and broke the absorption of your eye
as you lovingly kissed a morsel of that sweetest flesh
goodbye.

I pointed to a golden trickle
of butter running down your chin.
We dabbed our lips and smiled guiltily as if
it had almost been a sin

to lose each other
in this precious shared feast.
Then, leaning back, we let the waiter in
to pour out our last beer like an aproned priest.

Barges

I

The riverside air bears the sweetness
                of the first fallen blossoms;
magnolias bloom like supplicant hands.

II

Two thoughts take wing across the Hudson –
wings like a swan's that could break you.

III

We count 1 2 3 4 5 6 7 8 9 10 barges
and to each barge, another is lashed.

IV

My arm around you on the rusted railing,
we let them go like ten deep, black breaths.

Natural History

I

That scorching summer, while you worked,
I haunted the Natural History Museum, staring down
from a balcony of mandrill, koodoo and klipspringer
onto a herd of elephants mounted on an oval dais.

Across a landscape of familial shadows –
broad, proud foreheads, the slack helplessness
of haunches empty of power – two giant bulls
trumpeted mutely in the gloom.

I had a dream that each midnight, in this deep
pocket of silence, they were heard and a rich sap
spread through their bodies' thick bark.
Their trunks were first to thaw –

tired arms swinging back into circulation –
then ears like ragged kites beat the still air,
till, with imperceptible slowness, their barrel-
bodies swayed, bumped and jostled

as they climbed down – neat on their feet
as circus animals – onto the polished marble floor.
Their lily-pad footsteps echoed
in the great hall long after

they had left the nocturnal bongo
hiding in bamboo, the solitary okapi of the Congo
at ease in its cross-section of home.
And as they roamed past the ghostly light

each moribund culture, each threatened habitat
gave out, they sensed the grasslands of Central Park;
the dirt-tracks cool in the humid night –
living roots and the welcome of water.

II

Meanwhile, in your obsolescent white freezer
with its sticky door, four tea-bags float in darkness.
Screwed down in a litre glass jar, like drowned mice,
their labelled tails trail down the damp neck.

Each bleeds its own tangy spores, billowing
down like smoke, till the clear water grows brackish
and the flavour full of a slight bitterness
I can never quite get used to.

Below this totem – as I see it – plebeian,
uncomplicated, my six-pack (one down) gathers
its silver moisture. This sodden Scottish summer,
I still feel that first coldness –

each precious bead! – burn my fingertips, still hear
the early evening chink of your ice cubes,
the says it all *zitz* of my Bud.
I stare from the Crags down

into the bowl of Holyrood and am hit by the sour,
damp waft of the brewery (an animal smell like must
from a mass of thick-haired follicles). I see you
arriving home tonight, putting on the fans,

cupping the sluggish air in your bottom lip
and blowing. Across the white line of cockroach-
killing boracic acid, you tug that adhesive door.
As the light hums on and the cold hits your face

and you reach for that tall dark jar, perhaps –
past your tanned and trembling arm – an eye just catches
the opaque plastic hoop of a solitary, dislodged Bud
and you sense, withdrawing from it, the ghostly

after-image of a hand. Now, now do you feel
my elephants – free at last – pass behind you,
casting their great chill shadows
of longing and of loss?

The Years

Sometimes to get their own back
our years forget us. They uncouple
and trundle off, one by one,
down gentle gradients into sidings
overgrown by giant hogweed,
there to become their own
secret memorials.

Strange creatures take up residence
in the dusty old carriages –
shiny black beetles, tenacious fungus, a dwarf.
In faded photographs, seaside towns shift
mysteriously abroad.

Still – if you're lucky – rendezvous
can take place. Behind the mighty
blind engines of passion
may come tenderness – the freight
of the years.

from *The Moth Trap*
(1990)

In Old Galloway

Turf was torn from rich earth
and laid on poor; a wealth
of dykes conjured up
the steepest slopes – till a green
democracy was everywhere.

On bright summer evenings,
grasslands lit from within,
where would a child not go?
Up the hawthorns, over the hill
to Away! Of course, it's a lie:

this land too is rucked
with the bones and blood
guide books never chart.
In early spring, we pluck
little white knuckles from rich
dark moss – the kind that lines
the more comfortable
contours of our hearts.

Ghosts I

The upholding of the right in question was documented in 1726.

Remember I told you
of the ancient right
once claimed by the sparling fishers
of Minnigaff – that during the fishing
they may sleep in the bed
in the farm kitchen of Machermore
with whatever woman is there; the woman
being unclothed and no indecency
being committed.

Well, it gave me ideas
for insomnia. Now I have
a burgeoning night-time career.

No more for me memory's frozen rump;
no more thrashing in the white wilderness –
it is not a way to sleep
or to live. I prefer the warmth
of a stranger's bed.

Perhaps lately you have felt
my presence with you? –

though I have learned poise, stealth,
the value of stillness so well,
I can slip between the sheets
without the hint of a draught
touching you.

I like to feel a breathing body
next to mine: the heart pumping,
blood moving, the lungs
receiving, sending blood forth
transformed.

I am not alone
in liking to share such movements –

though they may seem
insubstantial to you;
ghostly as the flounder-trampers
we watched that summer evening
from high on the grassy fort.
Children they were, far out
on the unbroken fields of sand.

Remember I told you
they were the ghosts
of drowned fishermen
and that night you woke in panic,
your heart in the despairing clutch
of cold, rough, absent hands.

Ghosts II

'It's like dung in the teeth of my lover;
the knowledge that each night I must cower
in this small bed, while a stranger lowers
himself down and tugs at the covers.

It's then I feel the rough cloth stiffen
my nipples – this, the first stolen gift –
and, as a membrane between us, graft
together hearts that are barely living.

Yet *his* salt-heart still pumps like bellows
the slow blood's tired passage to his lungs;
and, with it, all I've held precious flows
into a midden of corrupted song.

Pet farm dogs twitch now by the dying fire
and the world shrinks within four thick walls.
I listen to the winds bind Machermore
to a darkness tighter than any laws.

From a grassy hill once, I watched ghosts –
flounder-trampers, far out on fields of sand.
They come to me now like fishermen lost
in the waters of sleep they fear most.

It's from such desperate hands I turn;
from a language I'd rather not learn.
But lover be quick! My body is milk
souring in a tall, cold churn.'

The Trader

'October 3rd (1831), when the disease (cholera) reached its culminating stage, was market-day; but when death was mercilessly tithing the town, no business toll was levied at the bridge. Out of nearly sixty carriers only one made his appearance.'

McDowell's *History of Dumfries*

I

Never could he forget that day
(the innocent beginnings
like rituals, unquestioned
as breath), when he crossed
the hump-backed bridge, his produce
no longer heavy on his back.
From the brow of the hill
he'd looked on the town
as an oil-board panorama
two thirds sky –
a badly weathered sky
whose varnish had been too thick
and darkening had gone hand-in-hand
with time's quotidian cracks.
This was the first omen
of ill: 'a dull, heavy film
altered the sun's rays
from bright gold to a lurid orange
mantling the town
in its shadow'. Such that
at the foot of the board –
equally dark – on the scroll
of the river might be written:
Watch therefore for ye know
neither the day nor the hour.

Even in old age
he terrified children
talking of the Great Pestilence;

for each simple brush stroke
remained separate and clear:
a dab of white –
a dead gull's wing, floating
down the river.
                    And yet
he could never explain
what had made him
walk towards that silence,
inhabit that darkness
in the tight fist of the town,
where air was rank
with the thick black smoke
of burning tar and pitch;
where everyone's nightmare
was the croak of *vox
cholerica* – the dusky-blue tinge
of death; where between cracked voices
there was even relish
for the equalising power
of death.

Years later they said
water was to blame –
that the river, swollen
with mud and refuse had quenched
yet contaminated the whole town.
But sweet reason
could not account
that he came back
a changed man – as if
something in himself
had been confirmed
and he knew time
would never shift it.

Thereafter, on all his travels,
what he liked best
was not travelling, not arriving,
but finding a small space
on a coach, a cabin, a chair –
a hard-fought space – where

II

in the half-dark of a chill autumn morning,
the early ground still pocked with mist

a young man is wiping tiny feathers
stuck with shit from warm brown eggs

placing each egg carefully between
layers of golden straw. And these

are movements there is no leaving
(the casual wave to his wife, framed

in the kitchen door), movements
that require the utmost concentration

for he must not break a single one;
movements that in the endless

repeating – over and over and over –
attain the forgetful purity of prayer.

The Death Mask of Robert Smith

Robert Smith was hanged in Dumfries on 12 May 1868 – the last public execution in Scotland. Askern was the hangman. Smith's death mask is in Dumfries Museum.

'There's no art / To find the mind's construction in the face.'

Shakespeare, *Macbeth*

I

Not sleep. Neither the brief, fugitive sleep
of Cain, nor that from which his warders
could barely shake him. More like the moment
a head's dragged up out of water, when hair's
plastered back, eyes blind, lips ready for breath.
His are lop-sided – sign of a final,
choking drool; for Askern, the dandy – dressed
more for a wedding than hanging – has bungled.
The head itself is narrow and the features
so ordinary – the small ears pinched in
at the top, nose just slightly off-centre –
it's a landscape with next to no bearings.
Nothing to draw from us a purity
of hatred or anger – even pity.
Pity for him? Nineteen and stocky-strong,
he coaxed Thomasina Scott (eleven)
into the dismal firs of Crofthead Wood;
raped her, strangled her, stole from her the clutch
of coins she'd been given for messages.
We stare, but the head stays a mildewed map,
washed by light – yielding nothing. And again,
it seems, we're stumbling around in the dark.

II

This evening
on the train, as light
fades and fields,
roads, houses

meld into blackness,
I pass
the dark arm
of Crofthead
Woods and think
of this again.
Sticks beat
through trees
the Sabbath
after the murder –
another cold,
winter's day.
Wind whipped in
from the Solway
across flat,
fallow fields.
Horses brushed
dry twigs
aside; shouts
rang out,
as scores of men,
women and children,
set free
from worship
after one short,
earth-bound
prayer, chased
the chill from the day,
smelled the hunt,
were scoured
by their own fear.

III

And the same Sabbath morning, *he* is found
at Kirk's Lodging House, Dumfries, enjoying
a pipe of tobacco, coolly dandling

a favourite child on his knee: Tell me,
what does all this clumsiness mean? His trail,
not so much clues as signposts –

the knees of his britches still bloody,
his naked wrists scratched; in his pocket
a handkerchief 'wet with blood' they tell it

as if horrified Nature had foregone its laws.
Does he see these damp walls as his Gethsemane? –
while back there – fifteen short miles –

they chip bits from the tree where she was found,
as if it is the Devil's Rood or next best thing
to chipping out his hazel eyes.

Do you know, in the dim lantern light,
to begin with, they could not tell
what had killed her? Shock –

or loss of all the thick, dark blood
that glazed her frozen thighs,
that clotted her hairless slit.

IV

Then it was, sometime after his 'full
and free confession', that they almost came
to love him: Robert Smith, orphan, bastard,

homeless, loveless, neither knower nor giver
of excuses for his muck of a life. A man drunk
on all he'd dreamed of evil, writing now

to the witness whose throat he'd tried to slit,
'Give my kind love to all the neighbours,
to your son John and to all the broom men;

and tell them that I will not see none of them
on earth, but I trust God I will see you
and yours and them in heaven.'

V

Come May – a wet and dismal morning – up against
the barricades in Buccleuch Street,

many of the six hundred turn their backs
and run. Those who stay

sigh deeply at each sorry stage
of ritual. But those who – at the last –

cut him down, after he has choked and kicked
for fully nine minutes (Askern, you bastard);

those who get close, as we can, must see
that for him – if not for you, if not for me –

Death is some kind of Baptism. Robert Smith
no more, they carry him shamelessly in their arms.

Galloway Tale

He told the map men anything.
But in Gaelic. That stretch
of bog? Old woman's fanny.
The small rise? Mharie's tit.

The maps were all printed
before he was rumbled: an ageing
hill shepherd – what did he
want of the outside world?

Provisions perhaps. Tools. A wife.
Each market day for two years
he wooed her (his fistfuls
of violets bound up with wool),

till – drunk as a lord –
after the market, after the wedding,
he took her back to the bald hills,
the gurgling-sounding places.

Years later, children were seen,
fetching water from dark pools,
cupping curlews' eggs. It's said
they fixed you with brown eyes,

sharp as kestrels', hovered
momentarily – and were gone
behind a line of dogs conjured
from the green ruff around

the thick-walled bothy. A slum
in the heather – so some saw it –
black pans lying unscoured, ropes
of washing rotting in damp piles.

When she died, he carried her
over the hills, over the burns,
on his back. At her graveside,
in the rain, he mourned on alone,

while in the pub, they put on
prim cartographer faces
and muttered that the loneliness
of earth would suit her.

from The Gift of Sight

Saint Medan

That Medan was beautiful,
    there was no doubt.
Wherever she went,
    hearts were routed.

But, to her, these looks
    were but a costume
she couldn't cast off.
    She saw her fortune

not in the fancy
    of romantic play –
it was in inner things
    her interests lay.

Medan took a vow
    of chastity; her life
she bound to Christ.
    It was a sharp knife

in the hearts of men.
    But one noble knight
did not believe her.
    To quit his sight

she left Ireland
    for green Galloway.
To the Rhins she came
    to live in poverty.

The knight followed.
    He would die or wed
his heart's crusade.
    Pure Medan now fled

to a rock in the sea.
　　　　With prayer, the rock
became a boat;
　　　　the boat she took

thirty miles away.
　　　　Still, he followed;
blindly obeying
　　　　what the hollow

in his heart called for.
　　　　He'd have been lost,
but a crowing cock –
　　　　to both their costs –

told him the house
　　　　where Medan lay.
Shaken, she climbed
　　　　and she prayed

as she climbed
　　　　into a thorn tree.
From there, she asked,
　　　　'What do you see

in me to excite
　　　　your passion?' 'Your face
and eyes,' he replied.
　　　　She sighed, 'In which case . . .'

then impaled her eyes
　　　　on two sharp thorns
and flung them at him.
　　　　Desire was torn

forever from that knight.
　　　　He looked at his feet,
where the eyes had rolled –
　　　　lustrous jade, now meat

for ants. Horror-struck,
        he left – a penitent.
Medan washed her face,
        for a spring – heaven-sent –

gurgled from the dry earth.
        The rest of her days
were lived in poverty
        and sanctity. (*Praise*

the Lord, sang Ninian.)
        The proud cock half-lived,
but crowed no more.
        And sight became the gift

Saint Medan gave,
        so that all could suffer,
in equal measure,
        beauty and terror.

Dry Stane Dyke

At the top of the twisting road
leading out of Glenkiln, please stop.

(You're going to have to anyway,
to argue whose will be the job

of opening the cattle-grid gate.)
Before you the Galloway hills

fan out across the horizon.
Follow each green peak, till your eye falls

to your right, to a bare, gently
sloping hillside, where a stone dyke

snakes its headless way, like a line
Paul Klee has taken for a walk

or a child's lasso that's missed all
but one cloud-shadow and two trees

and lies in bracken, abandoned.
Surely no lawyer drew up deeds

to protect what's here, to deny
what isn't; surely those who laboured

with rock upon rock upon rock
up the hillside, didn't favour

these distant curves for their own sake.
Brecht has pointed out History

records only the names of kings
as Thebes' builders – a mystery

how *they* hauled so many great lumps
of rock! Neither instigator

nor workers are remembered here,
on wall plague, stone or fine paper;

yet that kink at the far right end,
a lazy toe might improvise,

makes a mouth, that gives the whole
a fish-iness, that to my eyes

more than song, arch or tower, tells
of the playfulness of power.

The Moth Trap

In the centre of the sloping lawn, light
from the moth-trap floods the garden – surreal,
as if thought walked a green ceiling and sight
in such strangeness became a matter of feel.

The cut-out trees, the black teeth of a fence
mark the limits of this ordered landscape;
gleaming on the horizon its last defence –
the even lights of a runway, roped

across the night. Two fat poplar hawks thud
dully against glass along with a smirr
of lesser life: creatures not of blood
or substance, their death – a silvery smear.

A meagre haul this, till two boys tilt
into light, to match elastic shadows
and faces white as saucers of milk.
Each new element they dive in draws

a measure of proof. And so we observe
one the light calms, the other light excites;
one's a campfire Indian, the other's nerves
are taut, conscious of the wider night.

The light gives his naked movements the grace
of a wild boy reared on the forest floor.
Clothing them with laughter, he lifts his face –
there is nothing yet that can't be shared.

'Isn't childhood . . . ?' But I have answered yes
before you finish, still feeling the impress
of something wounded but wonderful
beating inside me against the darkness.

Frogs

Like someone strapped to a life buoy,
you lead me to the cottage door.
'Are you sure you'll be all right?
I must have a torch somewhere.'

I see the path by the hall light,
middling-muddy in the falling rain;
the gate a gap in the broad hedge.
I grope my way, call out, 'I'm fine.'

Halfway to the gate already,
with our last goodnights, the faint light
of the kitchen window guides me
to where the darkness seems complete –

the farm-track that leads to the road.
Here everything growing is black:
the central spine of tufted grass,
the hedge-wall, the cut-out trees flocked

with glimmering drops of rain.
The earth I walk on seems almost
metallic – a thin strip reaching
depths of darkness I cannot trust.

Yet the black is not so black,
when I recall the embers of haws,
the bright, wet coals of blackberry
this blind hedge, in daytime, grows.

And I feel, glowing within me,
the world I have left: the warm fire
of yet another receptive house,
where Alex, with bright purple hair

drains the last of the berry-red wine
and laughs as she paints us her life;
while Evan wraps himself in a book
and you smile through old pain and new love.

Easy to be there, to talk through –
with intelligence and feeling –
all the losses we need to grow;
so that, in time, the precious few

unmuddied thoughts I have seem huge.
Later, driving home on the twisting roads,
my headlights catch tiny wet frogs,
leaping like electrified pods

of seaweed over black tarmac,
as though their short lives are at stake.
And I have it! that breathless excitement –
the world before its waters break.

First Rites

Once again, it is the first night
of some good thing. Yet in this room
    sleep still can't know it –
sidling through, cagey as the moon:

at best we'll meet her at first light.
Till then, we lie in the darkness,
each, in thought, knowing the other's
    sleeplessness, yet holding
to stillness beneath the covers,

lest a brute world of feeling press
in and crush us. This is what I
am thinking (a thought the slight wind
    through the scaffolding
of trees has given me – the wind

which falls with a liquid sigh):
if I can't have sleep, then let me
have rain. I want to hear the rain.
    At first, a few drops
and then, those same few drops again,
till someone turns a giant key

and the heavens open. No blame
for you in this, my love: my ways
    are mysterious
(or weird) to us both. But come, let's praise
the rain; on this first night, it might tame

our just unease. For, with early light,
a darker awakening comes
    with a stag battering
his antlers against the wire drum
of the fence; the finger-tips bright

with blood – an angry stain, which spreads
over them, till the fence itself
      bears a thin, red shield.
Never will he see his true wealth
through our eyes; so why watch him wed

his beauty to violence
till dirty rags of skin hang down
      – softest velveteen –
draped each side of his bloody crown
and the fence rings in the silence?

One of the Beaten, you'd think, now
he slams into the wire once more;
      yet something in him knows
where he is going, that the gore
is but a blessing on his brow –

is where his strength has been planted.
As we watch, he and the blood-light
      of our geraniums
blur. A red tinge edges our night,
till a key turns and a wish is granted.

The Flower

Glandore, Co. Cork

I find you gone –
as you said you would – a walk
alone in the early morning
and to get a paper. Strange then –
in this, your first absence –
not to be thinking
of complications; to pose
the testing questions: *How
exactly do you feel? What's
the next move from here?*

Or to rise from this crumpled bed
and pad, bare-foot,
catlike around each
empty room, breathing
easy, as your postcards
and toilet bag lie
open-mouthed before me.

Such thoughts would make
you shake your head.
'Funny man, you are.
Funny man.' Yes,
just lying here, arms
akimbo, sensing
my life hum in the silence.

I picture your busy
clockwork walk
round the still coves.
The silver water barely
ripples as you launch the first
hopeful skiffy stone
into the bay. Two skips
and all human warmth
is washed from it. Memory
too has done with it. (But when
you stoop to recall
yesterday's names
of tormentil and thrift,
the red-tipped claw
of bird's foot trefoil
snags on your mind.)

And now I almost feel it –
your hair falling in my face
when you bring me coffee,
a paper and a wildflower
that's new to us both.

It is that moment I wish
I could hold to: the unnamed
flower between us,
turning in my fingertips,
washed by our mingled breaths –
a room for our eyes to live in.

How close
will we get
to this flower
before it burns
like any other
patch of colour?
Here, let it
turn in our eyes'
thirst to know it
as it now is
in all its fragile
delicacy,
its short-lived
perfection.
    And turn
one more time,
before I reach
for the book to name it –
if it should have a name –
and you take it
and carefully
place it
and press it.

The Foxglove

Source of the drug digitalis, which is used to treat heart ailments.

I

Nothing tame about
the foxglove that grew
by that cottage stream.

More like a tall fir
or proud cypress than
flower, but wild and

not waving, but swaying
its coat o' bells in strong
summer breezes. Once

it would have stood
no chance to stay
so tall: the hand

that stripped docken
and fingers of fern,
that waged open war

on all things taller
than grass, smaller than
a tree, with a good stick,

would have brought it
crashing down in a blur
of bruised and broken

blossoms – a panic
of feasting bees. (See
its stringy stalk still

joined by a few green
umbilicals – the rest
ruined, utterly.)

But it grew way past
the end of my growing,
my lust to see the tall –

in nature – fall.
Both its time and spot
were well-chosen.

II

A secret track leads
from the cottage door
to a short tumble

of water and a clear,
cool basin, now choked
with forbidding broom.

This lies just below
the ford,
    where years before,
the waters in spate,

the farmer made a bridge
of an old, broken
trailer-top. The backboard

he cast aside
in tufted grass
to bloom with lice.

There it has weathered,
till the wood is grey
and mossed as rock –

a strength that lies;
for through its broken back
the foxglove had thrust.

(What a clean swipe
it could have been!
I felt the shocked itch

of the limbless.)
         That week
in idle routine, I'd
walk over to peer

down a spotted throat,
past the lip of sparse,
white stubble, designed

to keep the needless
out. The yellow sacks
of pollen clustered

on the flower's roof,
fresh as morning rolls,
on the curving ends

of milky tendrils.
Or – thoughtfully – I'd
sleeve a few fingers

with any seamless,
lilac softness that
had already fallen.

The onion-domed
seedcases themselves,
fat and shining-green –

the point of the staff –
were waiting for time
and a little sun

to lean on them. The tip
of the foxglove curved –
a tender probe or

question mark. Still,
even if I stood
at its base and shook

till I was buried
in all its blossoms,
what could that foxglove

tell, but of itself?
There have been nights –
far from it – when

I've dreamed I sit
on the rotting fibres
of that board and clutch

the foxglove like a mast.
The wind slaps leather-
leaves against me,

seedcases explode
at last above me;
yet I remain calm

for I have taken
the foxglove's medicine:
my heart grows strong

and I don't even wake
now, when I feel
the deep roots loosening.

On Arran

Five deer, we'd thought
fenced in with sheep,
tamed with lush, lowland grass,

within reach of hawthorns
and the sea, appear on the road
and, from a standing jump, flow

over the wire fence
into the opposite field,
into a contrary landscape,

like water poured
from one glass into another.
By the time we've locked the car

and got over the stile,
someone's moved them way up
the green hillside. They stand

close, but too neatly –
a give-away grouping – arranged
by some childish, godlike hand.

Then we are two parties –
the two parties of the glen –
they always a little higher,

a little ahead, vaulting
through the landscape, not even
touching the heather; as we,

contrary beings, it seems
seep with each new step
further into a banking of mud

and sedge smoothed flat
after a full winter's wet.
They stop now and stare us out

across the mountain stream.
Sniffing, their elegant heads
assume a natural aristocracy;

while we, clumsy but bright
savants of the mountains,
wave and shout them on:

'You've come thus far;
now we are the life –
the life of Glean Easan Biorach

and you must stay with us –
at least to the cold, blue heart
of Loch na Davie, to the very edge

of the grey mist rolling
down Cir Mhor. We seek signs
of companionship, not judgement.'

*

We scour the hillside,
but they've become so many
heathery streaks between scree.

Of course, I think that later.
For the moment, I stand with you,
coated in the soft, island rain,

and stare and stare
over the empty, glacial valley,
till you say, 'Well, can you

spot them then? Can you?'
But what is there to answer you
that is not root, water or rock?

Casey's

Glandore, Co. Cork
Casey's looks over the bay and its islands – Adam and Eve.

At last, as the creamy clouds of Guinness
slowly settled, he acknowledged that today
was a *bad* day. His face – a Barry Fitzgerald
of crumpled kindness – peered with us

at the drizzle filling the bay of Glandore.
The hazy wedges of Adam and Eve
were dark-grey smudges on the smudgy sea.
Yesterday – warmer, but with a mist thick

as a West Cork accent – we had stood
and stared out at a safety curtain
that had never risen on the day. 'Still,
not a bad day,' opined Larry Casey,

fourth generation owner of *Casey's*
three-and-a-half-centuries-old bar; now
more given to tourists than fisherfolk.
That first night, Adam and Eve were sharp-edged

as anvils at the head of the bay.
'A mile apart,' Mr Casey told us,
his tone assured of our quizzical 'No!'
'Yes. And once they used to lie side by side.

But since the terrible sin that cast us all
from Eden, God has made them ever lie
so far apart.' This told with a slight smile:
it was a gift of whose worth he was sure.

But when customers talked, Mr Casey
withdrew to a quiet seat near the bar.
Snippets of conversation fell to him:
'Where there's children, there's life – don't you think?'

'Ah yes,' came the soft voice round the corner,
'tis lovely to be innocent.' The last night,
we talked of the Glandore Regatta.
'Tis a pity you're going, right enough –

tis a fine day, the Glandore Regatta.
Still, if you've got the time, you shouldn't miss
the view above Loch Ine. Yes, I tell all
the visitors about it, for it is –

to my way o' thinking – the most beautiful
spot in Ireland.' His small, guiding hands curved
round many roads; spidered up the hillside.
'Here you can take a little rest. And here . . .'

While outside, only the sea mist hugged Eve,
as the sailing manuals told it, and the rain
– that tireless step-dancer – kept on trying
to douse ten thousand beams of fuchsia.

Visiting the Poet

for Norman MacCaig
(after Akhmatova's tribute to Aleksandr Blok)

When I visit the poet,
when is not important.
It's the same firm handshake;
then whisky, water and glasses.

The city can be grey and cold;
his walls are stoked against it:
landscapes, friends; spines/spines/spines
and flame-haired faces.

My host is never silent for long –
interrupts with a look
if my language is loose, for his talk
is as honed as his writing.

I remember a conversation
we had once. I wrote it down later.
Like most of our talks,
it concerned poetry.

He told me: You must have faith
that there's water in the well;
trust your ear; pick up a pen
at the slightest nudging.

And lastly – hours or minutes
from my arrival – he told me:
'Remember this: You never know what
you may do tomorrow.'

Good advice, don't you think? –
even when set down on the cold page
without the warmth of whisky
or the conviction of a lifetime.

Russian Still-life

Kiev to Moscow sleeper

Though the signs are of sleep,
neither one of us has slept.
The rocking train has kept
us awake, till the pale light seeps
through the rucked blue curtains.
Both our pillows lie crushed,
points twisted in a rush
of anger. But nothing gained
ignoring day, we've pulled
at half the blue and swiped
our damp breath away. Light
from the orange sun – cool
as Vermeer – paints the rims
of tea-glasses silver,
makes the spoon's tip quiver.
Four tea-bags weep in the dim
of the saucer, like dank,
old leaves. Augurs of day:
your rolled tie; the way
that towel offers its blank
image, waiting for a face.
Tall birch trees shimmer past.
Lit from behind, they mask
great fields that show no trace
of all the blood that made them.
They are ploughed silences -
the horizons, their fence.
And, before the station's mayhem,
I note this last down:
flowers in a curved vase,
whose small heads are scraps of lace
torn from the fading moon.

from *Red Letter Day*
(1996)

Loving, Writing

If your love was true
and you lose it, what have you lost?
Not the act of loving. That's yours.

If your words were true
and you lose them, what have you lost?
Not the act of writing. That's yours too.

In loving, in writing, how can you
hold onto a finished thing? Whether
you lose it or put it beneath glass,

it is the act itself you must cherish.
For what's left when the moment has passed,
the wind will carry. Despite you.

New World Dreams

'... deep surroundin' darkness
Is aye the price o' licht.'
                        Hugh MacDiarmid

I

Arrived safely. But already too late.
I rummage through bottomless chests of maps,
straighten the bleeding crucifix, make up
tales to fit the tapestries. A cool room
with an arched veranda's been prepared.
Sun burns through honeyed stone; the moveless air
never clears its hot reek of burning flesh
and native women. Their dark eyes hate us
or they die. (There is a novel in me;
its pages weigh me down like coffin lead.)
I stare over harbour and sparkling sea.
I spin the globe. Find Eldorado, I say.
Drive on! Find the counterweight to balance
all this suffering, boredom and death.

II

Out of deep surrounding darkness, a globe
of Borgesian exactitude. It glows,
though parts of its surface are dark-edged, furred
with jostling moths. *Lacrimae addicta.*
Throughout the dry seasons of history
they have swept through the forests and savannahs
of Africa, Asia, America.
Fastening on the most placid creatures
or the most weak, they worry the eyeball
then gorge on the salt-licks of their tears.
No one's ever starved feeding on suffering,
sadness and pain. Spin the globe. See! Rainbows
arch over the giant cataracts
they have made. Bright blue butterflies dance there.

III

Take a hammer to the night. Rake over
the glittering shards. The stage-set plaza
with its crumbling delicacy, violence
throbbing down the alleys. From dark doorways
the calls: 'Good marijuana, good mari . . .'
'Eh gringo! Wan' fuck you over the moon.'
('Careful, mister, these people not your friends.')
In a cafe so open it hovers
in the velvet air, a lusty negra
thrusts the pink throttle of her tongue at me:
it has wings like a bird or the flowers
one feeds on. Fear and desire: these you must pass
to the lone singer's resigned, happy songs.
'We are here,' one song says. 'We are here.'

IV

What once lived here lives on in the outskirts,
the hot outback. ('They'll skin you alive,
mister' – crimson your face with chicken blood.)
Stay with the church, the bars and the music.
Let the golden beer cool you and the hawkers
move among you: nuts, roses, a statuette
of a saint. And more insistently
the beggars: the rheumy-eyed kids, the youth
hauling his eloquent stumps through the dirt,
the hopelessness of the old. Eat and drink.
This is the world. Rest assured, this is the world.
Before it slips from your grasp with its ghosts,
choose. It is our privilege and mild pain
to bless dead eyes with arbitrary coins.

Miss Killough

Source: one of Elizabeth Bishop's letters

Old friends know best
to give me space. Take Lota, my old school chum,
content to leave me for hours soaking
in this deep bath, listening
to Dona Elizabetchy's old Corona
clacking away like an angry remonstrance.
Though the poems of hers I've seen are perfect,
clear as water, the clack clack clack
of these sharp black tongues
takes me back
to the operatic rows
between Mama and Miss Killough.
For days they'd build up, Mama muttering
under her breath at Miss Killough's
coolly appraising eye, becoming ever more
agitated till she was tented
in silence as the thunder brewed.
The smallest incident triggered the storm:
Miss Killough pointing out, 'Senhora,
it does the girls no good to see you
snacking so.' Or, 'Well, Senhora,
even though it is carnival, I think
in this you go too far.'

And I see them before me
still trapped in the languages
which made them, Mama's arms flailing
with her tongue, 'O Sacco de Jesus!
a thousand curses on me – but . . .' as she stamps
round the room lifting and laying books, letters,
trinkets; Miss Killough simply growing taller,
whiter, more thin-lipped. 'Well, Senhora
I'm sure I've no wish to stay
where I'm not wanted.' And in the silence
which follows, the creak of her steamer trunk

and the dull thwacks of heavy underwear
are the loudest sounds in Rio.

Still as a candle, Mama now holds
the centre of the room, flickering at us
with her pale flame of a face. First
at my sister then at me. 'Maria Cecilia,
what do I do with such a woman?' I shrug
hopelessly. 'Then so be it!
Let her go back to her precious Aberdeen.'
But we both know Mama will soon
be knocking on Miss Killough's door
and begging a pardon Miss Killough
will readily give. For in truth what has she
to go back to? By all accounts a cold grey city
that stinks of fish – though she always
talks of it fondly, always says
she'll never get used to the heat.

Next morning, as if nothing had happened,
we'd have a bowl of oatmeal
(as I still do) and set off for our daily walk.
The Botanical Gardens, early,
were her favourite: royal palms
and hummingbirds. Rarely the beach.
'A lady should be pale,' Miss Killough
used to say. 'I want no part in raising
bothy quines.' But she smiled in saying it.
I still carry her picture
in my prayer book, looking as I imagine
a Scotch Highlander does – thick with tweeds
and with a firm expression that says,
'Maria Cecilia, I know what's best for you.'

At forty-five I'm still regarded
as something of a beauty in this city
of beautiful woman: smooth skin, perfect teeth,
a blond mane and, for interest's sake,
as Miss Killough used to say, one brown eye

and one blue, bright as a hummingbird
in the dark. A thoroughbred
I move through the city's moneyed heart
as keen a student as any of the hierarchies
of blood our history's composed of. Yet
fifteen years after her death, I hear
her Rs like waves rolling through my speech
and find myself turning
from those English salon ladies who spurned her;
or saying to my patriotic hosts, 'Oh
this hopeless country! It's a wonder
anything gets done.'

To her hopeless charges
she left all her little money, even took
to their religion just before she died.
She said her own church seemed cold to her;
in her last days she wanted something more friendly
than bare stone walls. 'Maria,' she said
at the end, 'it's a bonnie name.'

None of us had seen her
softening. How could the edges
of her hard country blur with ours?
Or more remarkably Scotland's grey charms
enter our souls. But I carry
her exile within me as well as
the aches and pains of deportment I try
to soak away. So I have one blue eye
on Rio, the other – the brown –
on Scotland's flinty shores.
In Nossa Senhora da Candelaria
I light a candle for her
whenever I can. I always look
on the painting of Antonio de Palma surviving
the shipwreck, but it's Miss Killough
I see raising her skirts
to climb ashore.

First Night in the Tropics

The sun bronzed
the palm-fronds
and disappeared.
Took with it
everything. Even
snuffed the egrets
that rode like tall
white candles
on the cattle's altar-
backs. The road
came to mean
kerosene lamps
and someone rocking
in a roadside shack;
figures walking
that were darkness
thickening, that night
snatched back
again. The path
was 'Cuidado, boys!
Cuidado!' Roots.
Rocks. Water.
Was a false trail
of fireflies –
now here!
now there! –
in the thick maze
of air. And that night,
past the neat
village that slept
in its hollow beneath
the salt-spilled sky,
I caught sight of
the bright green
sliver of a lizard

shinning up a wall –
a watchstrap
with no watch
and no need; for the time –
less days stretched out
there, in the long darkness,
ready to match
my vision of them –
a long string
of precious stones
being polished
by the pounding sea.
I saw the perfect
breathless
crescent of sand
(it was! it was!),
a fringe of dense
coconut palms
leaning towards
limpid, blue light;
and every piece
of flotsam waited –
even as warm rain
in a single sheet
drove down – to sing
like a crickets' chorus:

> *Make me*
> *into a cup, a pestle,*
> *a fruit bowl . . .*
> *Why not*
> *live here*
> *always?*

The Find

'Are there Spaniards in heaven? Then light the fire.'
Enriquillo, Taino freedom fighter

After the great storms
which dyed the sea dark red
and left the piled coconuts
like a massacre of bearded skulls
along the beach, there is
a calmness in the village tonight –
a fresh space, which is open
to possibility. As if to match
something to the moment,
Cañete produces
a small brown object
and offers it in the palm
of his hand. It is a perfect
Taino axehead of dark
obsidian stone. He has found it
in the forest. 'This is what happens
when lightning strikes stone.'
'Yes,' says another,
I've seen it happen.'
We pass the stone
around our huddle, feeling
its cool smoothness
in our hands.
      As we look,
the group is joined
by a young man, who is soon
nodding agreement. 'Once
I saw a horse struck
by lightning,' he tells us.
'It just stopped
dead in its tracks.
I went up to it

and touched it
on its forehead.
Like this . . .' Delicately,
his fingers anoint
the silence.
'It collapsed
into a pile
of white ashes – right there
in the middle of the road.'

*

Yet not for long.
Soon it is back;
but this time, it is a horse
made from ashes
which stands before you
in the middle of the forest path,
as the sun makes the earth
steam around its grey,
ghostly legs. Go on,
touch it. It is yours now,
is it not? Touch it:
it will collapse again
and be nothing.
Yet how sure
seems its body
on its four pillars
of ash. It stands
in your mind more rootedly
than the lightning which killed it
or the storm of fires
in which Enriquillo
finally drowned.

Jungle Lover: A Letter

Today I walked deep into the humid heart
of a real, green jungle. And yes, you would
believe it, got lost. Though the fading sun

still played on the high canopy, for me
down below it was already too late.
At the slow, brown-bellied river I found

my first dead end. By then the crude map
was a pale glow in my hands. I'd as well
read the broad black leaves on the forest floor.

I didn't panic straight away. A lightening
of foliage gave – disappointingly early
I thought – some prospect of success.

But it was only a gash of sunlight
through a treefall the hungry canopy
had not yet closed over. The path led back

into the dark tunnel and I'll admit,
yes, to my first real twinge of panic then.
I start to jog along the faint grey light

of the wrong trail. I call out but the dense
foliage absorbs every sound I make
and returns silence. Deafening silence.

Vicious thorns snag me, roots trip me, tree trunks
slam into me. I stumble off the path
into closed darkness. Lost. Utterly lost.

Covered with sweat and insect repellent
(my one foresight) I wait, feeling strangely
calm now I know my efforts are hopeless.

One more black silhouette in the jungle,
I threaten nothing but sit on my branch,
attentive as all the creatures must be

which hoot, whistle and breathe in the stillness.
And slowly the forest reveals itself:
the cry of a bird, the crash of a branch,

the rustle of leaves as a small creature
moves through the forest litter. I too turn
nocturnal, one with the living darkness:

let the daylight find me. And find this letter too.
It will tell you of torchlit seekers
who never reach me, though we circle each other

like jaguars along the clotted paths.
At times I think I see the candlelights
of a lodge within reach – the warmth of food

and laughter, the tame macaw I wrote you of
that tried to crack my fingernails apart.
But some choice makes me snuff all of them out

to head back into this mapless green world
where I can feel closer to your heartbeat.
And everywhere I go the forest follows

flowing into my traces like the sea
into empty scoops of sand. Between the lines
of this letter, listen for the broken sounds

as one more ageless tree tires, falls and drowns.

For Big Tree

Big Tree is a strangler fig.

I walk the forest floor and rarely look up
from the light-hungry leaves, the fallen trees
rich with the fast-forward of tropical
decay, the militant lives of the ants.
But then I arrive at the great winged roots
of Big Tree and their slow, gentle curves say
Follow – into the smooth, thick trunk and up
to where the silver arteries are spread
with profit over the thick canopy.
Below, I stand in the deep, mossy shade
while up there small green arrows drink the last
sunlight. But Big Tree – tallest and proudest
in this forest – is not a tree at all.
Listen to its story.
                    A thumbnail seed
lands high on the trunk of a lapuna.
The wind takes it there or a choosy bird
wipes it from its beak. The seed germinates
and sends missionary roots to the thin
earth for nourishment. These roots grow. Do you
believe how these roots have grown? Now they flare
out into giant flanges to buttress
the new tree, enfolding the lapuna
which slowly withers within its casing.
But this new tree, this freak, dependent plant,
has not finished yet. Now it reaches high
above the lapuna's old crown. It clears
the dense, green canopy and emerges
into an infinity of blue light.

I like to stand by Big Tree between two
cool, hollow wings. Big Tree, *mi madre*,
I feel the sure spread of your roots. I feel

the good sunlight drunk deep within you.
I find it comforting to know what first
appeared as misfortune, time and effort
have transformed; that an old host, having played
its part, decays in favour of a fresh
green self, rooted in water and sunlight.

Voices: Four Meditations and a Lament

on words scratched on the windows of Croick Church in Ross-shire

1. *Glencal people was in the churchyard here*

From Maeshowe to Pompey; from Lascaux to Tobruk:
the ancient mark of momentary presence,
the signature of ghosts. With their absence they paid
for this gaunt landscape, those who sought shelter
in the churchyard, too pious to enter the church itself.
Lit by small fires in the damp, tented graveyard,
the peat-cutting hand cut into the glass. He signed
in another tongue to reach another shore:
they had been broken on their own, their name a song
already fading. I can still catch his breath
as fist and flint loop across the small diamond pane.
This is harder than breaking rocks! But it must be said.

2. *Murder was in the year 1845*

Call a spade a spade. There are many ways to skin
a rabbit and none knew more of them than they did.
First you must kill it. Deal in facts as the graveyard does:
birth, death – murder. This voice is the bitter whisper
in the wind: you can't shake it this end of the glen.
Though the murder written of here didn't happen here,
as the lament that sings in Wounded Knee was composed
many years before it, and the murder of Kurds
driven like deer was in someone's eyes long before it.

Savages all, bent over greenwood fires, despair
a field creature hiding in the dark litter of their eyes.
The Lord is our shepherd, but let the year not forget us –
each numeral painfully scored into the singing winds.

3. *Glencalvie people the wicked generation*

As if they were another species, someone
from *The Times* spoke for them to the wider world,
told of the wretched spectacle they'd made leaving
their land at last, refugees with carts of children,
the poor supporting the helpless poor. Anon wrote:
If such as happened here transpired in the south
there would be outrage. (His pen; their flint.) But they,
being damned, damned themselves. Though they grew like rowans
in the rock of the land, their spirits cracked
like firs without it. This voice is the saddest fiction
and they took it to the grave. The wretched of the earth –
shaking the journalist's hand, he thought, like children.

4. *Glencalvie is a wilders . . .*

Passing over a swell of lonely hills that sap
the earlier green of the strath, black cloud shadows,
like lids in the sky, close on clear runs of sunlight.
The rubble of an ancient broch can give no shelter here,
nor the ruined sheepfolds pinned to the hills.
The faint light still catches the last of their voices
muted by horse chestnut, sycamore and ash,
though the wind soughing through the tall spruce bites
back the last word. Their backs turn from you now, their carts
move off and they fade, leaving not the pristine world
of *Walden*, but a hard land that once gave shelter
turned into a land of ghosts, a wilders . . .

Coda: Lament

from the observations of a musicologist on an untranslated song
by an Aché Indian whose tribe faces systematic genocide in Paraguay

It is above all and beyond all doubt a doleful song,
characterised by a melismatic note, a monotonous tone,
appearing to involve a repetitive attempt
at a drone-like narration of some overwhelmingly sad
                               and disturbing events
which seem to have affected the home.

The singer's inner agitation is clearly shown
in the way his face appears drained and drawn,
with a fixed smile as ironic accompaniment
      for such a doleful song.

One is left with the lasting impression
of a man who has been battling with tears too long;
but who, even in exhaustion, cannot cease his lament.
His is the haunting voice of peoples whose futures are rent,
whose stolen past cannot come again.
      It is above all a doleful song.

In the Botanics: Edinburgh

An hour till dusk. The castle lodges its span
in the crook of a giant sycamore.
Through arteries of beech, the domes and spires
of the city turn to a scattered fan
of embers. I kick chestnuts from the path
and, like a bird scuttering through the black
skirts of a rhododendron, forage back
into my past. That's when your airy laugh
calls me. Maria Angeles Huarte,
your daughters share spirits with the squirrels
they feed, dancing between silver birch light.
You yourself know the moment's poetry:
'See!' the sooty heron's labouring flight,
the cypress where its wings stumble and curl.

Homers

The farmer's son in Kintyre
gave us four pigeons
at our holiday's end – two each
and we could choose, though not
the most dependable homers.

He scooped them from the rafters
of the outhouse above
the grey drills of shit. It took
two hands to hold one; one to lock
round its tail and feet

as the other calmed it,
calmed myself, running a finger
round the thick thumb
of its head, over a nutmeg-
speckled breast.

Home in Edinburgh
our neighbour had no problem
holding my two birds, one cooped
in each large fist. Poor homers –
lazy, unlucky or what? –

while I idled in the cool hut
waiting their coffin-lid
scratchings, he'd plucked them, feet
like roots, from his lime-green
rows of seedlings.

Voyagers, I'd thought them
and launched them from open palms
to gain blue and in great arcs to skim
some imagined geography
home. Tonight

the pigeons' heads poke
from our long-dead neighbour's fists
as tiny wavering flames
against the long shadow
of the hedge. We fly

always above open palms
and nothing brings us home.
It was weeks before I trusted
those pigeons again. And when I did
they were gone.

The Loch

I've found that loch again – the one
where I stand at autumn's edge
and look over a broken stretch
of tussocky grass, a handful
of young birch trees; and imagine

a clear sandy edge of water
before depth is lost to tangled
black weed, rhythms of stirred up silt.
Something breaks in the pine forest
beyond it – a dead branch? Or deer?

Two or three, moving down through firs
which darken to blue in the late
afternoon light: deer drawn down
through sweet-smelling pines, their hooves light
on the pine floor; deer drawn down to water.

A bird call fills the clearing then,
spreads out from its watery core.
Nothing else. I've never been here
before, so can't comprehend how
something quite so still, so complete-

ly of the moment, can carry
so many other lochs within.
Yesterday's art gallery held
another kind of stillness. Keen,
attentive as deer, people picked

their way between exhibits; each
pausing wherever they were drawn.
One man clapped a child to his chest
to share his vision: Goncharova's
Soldier in the Forest, Chagall's

The Poet Asleep. At each green dream,
he ruffled the hair of the child
with his lips, so that it stood up
there like a tuft of bog cotton.
Just before the evening chill breaks

my concentration, I feel lips
gently brush the base of my skull.
Somehow I have always felt loved.
Nothing says that in the picture
but it's there. In the darkness

firs rise from the nape of the loch,
the black roots of gathered up hair.
An early star burns needle sharp
at the forest's edge. With each light step
a bruised scent of pine fills the air.

Barn Dance

in the Central Belt

Horsey, horsey, don't you stop,
just let your hooves go clippety clop.

We take the mnemonic, but leave the dance,
the barn's store of stoorie warmth,
its whoops and giddy laughter.

'Want to see the calves?' Across
the muddy, moonlit yard is a shadow
the shape of a hangar.

Two calves rise from darkness there,
uncross themselves and straightleg it
to our still, cupped hands.

Once I taught calves to drink,
letting them suckle my fingers
in a bucket of milk. And now

you too will feel the light, damp
clamp of a mouth, the smooth bridges
of teeth, as one tawny calf

and one brown draw in everything
that inhabits this cool spacey air –
all but our awareness

of their sexual slurp. We sense,
more than see, our eyes smile. 'Tickles,
doesn't it?' 'Yes (a laugh) yes.'

I run my hand along the soft,
curved ridge of my brown's neck,
petting it. Oh, my city roots!

Down the lane, at the second bend,
where the music dies and the beaded lights
of an estate have us surrounded,

we nuzzle each other in the silence,
in the middle of this dark green lung.
Horsey, horsey, don't you stop!

We turn our hands, sniffing
our fingers, like the first people.
The milk of children is on them.

Night-Night

You take to bed early
these days. When I join you
you're already well away, face crushed
to the edge of the bed;
a great white booby bird
sniffing the muddy currents
from the wreck of papers,
slippers, hairdryer, books
etc. below your beak.
Or lying like a cartoon
character just as sleep
has ambushed you, open
pregnancy book tilting
from your fallen knees. (So
how many times have you read
that section on 'vomit'?)
Standing in the middle
of the room tonight, you
lift up your nightdress. 'Look,
they're getting bigger now' –
your breasts, growing like fruit,
marbled with thin blue veins –

the faintest hyacinth
tracery. I take their weight
on my hands and hold them
while you float on my tide
in the lamplight, the trees'
sloe-black hearts behind you.
Once upstairs you lead me
again through the keyhole
patterns of growth. 'And now
it's this size,' holding up
a pinky. I recall
among grey filings that
electric energy,
one Escher I can't lose
the sense of: a seed-sized
heart pumping as the legs
like fusewire lit from within
knitted furiously.

I'm not ready for sleep.
On the TV, tracers
stitch up the night sky
over lunar deserts;
men offer their lives like crumbs
on their fingertips, eyes
expecting no mercy.
Here, the barnacles honk
as their slow Vs pass us;
large, loose snowflakes launch
themselves at the window,
the wind giving their flight
a final tick. They land
with a touching lightness.
Whatever connects them
is lost in the darkness.

The Bathroom: Midnight

Not to waken you, I leave all lights off
to squat down amid the darker shadows
of all that in this shifting time we've brought
here: baskets, lamps, a fifties radio . . .

Like those washed-out landscapes you drive past, fast
in the night or the mist-drenched day: milky heads
of trees, the swell of buildings lying vast
distances over frosted fields, till the road

twists and farmhouse lights rush towards you.
Resting on chalky thighs, I try the weight
of what's to come beyond the faint grey-blue
edged trees, but taste only air and light.

And, as air grows thinner and light darker,
death becomes as clear as the cormorant
frozen at the weir, its spread wings blacker
than itself. My frail mother takes my hand:

'You are the sixth in line to bear your name.
Some day the grandfather clock will be yours.'
It anchored the bright galaxy of home -
once thought fixed – whose fractured light pours

over us. At its rim I can make out
the shining bone-white speck of an eggcup;
one of those still-life details by Van Eyck
that draws you close to the canvas to probe

how the eye can be convinced by a few
deft strokes of oil. But the eggcup remains
real in its realm as this basket with its (now)
waxen glow whose roughness will come with dawn.

For in the simple dawn all will be revealed:
the curve of the lamp, the chunky brown knobs
of the radio. Light will put the seal
on the whole Vuillard crush and objects mob

us like seagulls from their cramped surfaces
in their desire to be loved. We have made
our inheritance too, have made our place
from others' places. But connections fade

and sometime, my child, this jerry-built wing
will seem all for you. May you love it in all
its particularity – nothing wrong
with that – yet sitting in this crowded stall,

I think a landscape that also rings true
is the early one that looked so fragile
and washed-out. The one as children we rush through,
bursting through fields for mile upon mile

until up ahead with a welcoming glow
we see farmhouse lights shining on fresh snow.

Chinese

Lying in the bath
    I feel a light breeze
through the skylight
    graze my bare shoulders

and knees. I slip
    down lower and slap
warm water between
    gulches and sluices.

I shut my tired eyes.
    What a night last night!

And the moon Li Po
          would write home about.

From the bridge we watched
          as it rose over
the river and shone
          bright as any shield.

We could have touched it!
          I blink: Liberty's
on the toilet seat
          reaching for the skylight.

A moth's trapped there
          by the wooden frame,
its wings the faintest
          breath. Panic has sapped

its energy, so
          my wife flicks it free
then, panting, shuts off
          the draught from me.

In the final push
          the cord of her robe's
failed her and the globe
          of her stomach's lit

by the sun's last rays.
          Li Po lives again
in this final scene.
          Pale and dripping wet

he holds the full moon
          in his hands at last –
its heartbeat as breath
          on his shattered wings.

A Red Letter Day

Headline in the Glasgow Herald, 22 August 1991

I

The day you were born was 'A Red Letter Day'.
In the crumbling Empire, the forces of reaction
were sent packing; the Gang of Eight,
after their botched coup, fell on each other
'like cockroaches in a jar'. Stories abounded
of flight and of suicide. Yeltsin
was the hero of the hour: a Russian bear
padding along the terrace of his besieged White House
or roaring from a tank top: 'The honour and glory
of Russian men-at-arms shall not be stained
with the blood of the people.' Broodily determined
beneath his silver hair, there was yet something cruel
about his lips, something of the thrill and energy
of power in all his movements. While he appeared
as an actor Eisenstein might cast
in some shadowy Russian parable, off-stage
in the Crimea, Gorbachev ordered his own plain
potato face to be videoed, telling it as it was,
as he awaited his diminished return.

Now the tanks which the brave few had rushed
in the fevered television lights with tarpaulins
and wooden beams, whose barrels had sniffed
the air and known it forever changed,
were rolling down Moscow's boulevards
in triumphant retreat. 'The People Have Won!'
'The People Have Won!' Garlands and bouquets –
even numbers for the dead – piled up on the spots
where the three martyrs for freedom
had laid down their lives. Soon
we would all know the looming white faces
of these 'Heroes of the Soviet Union' –

one serious, one smiling, one Jewish.
'Forgive me, your president,' Yeltsin's voice
cracked, 'that I could not protect your sons.'
Already newly-weds visited their shrines
to bless their wedding days; for this was History
and happening so fast, like a great log jam
had broken and the pent up waters
of Freedom and Democracy were rushing
everywhere; with Tsarists shoulder
to shoulder with Anarchists who knew what
the new order would turn out to be.

Sitting alone in the changed world,
my excitement having given way
to a fluid calm, my vision,
even in the fading light, still sharp,
coating each object, as if my looking
conferred light, I cut the headline out.

On 'A Red Letter day', I watched a surgeon
thrust white hands deep into your mother's stomach,
scrabble about as if there were finishes touches
to be made – a bow to be tied, a feature kneaded
into shape – or as if he were simply gathering up,
this late summer, two handfuls of autumn leaves.
From the gallery, I held to that feeling
of the leaves holding together between my palms
(a few falling from the edges, but nothing
could break my concentration now) as I raised them
carefully up and up, the blood-smell of autumn
ripening in the air, till with a shout
they were over my head and released
into the wind. Pure joy! A dove
from red silken rags; a head, so
perfect, so beautiful. So it's true, love
can read the writing on the furthest star:
my eyes focussing with the intensity of heart,

body and soul. Then the body, in the middle
of this white, this green aquarium light, the body
a warm, a russet, a maple glow. Oh,
I saw you for us both, saw the beautiful boy
rising from his mother's innards, she spread,
spread and used like earth, as like a rose tree,
he seemed to rise by himself through the air,
his pulsing stem the cord rooted
in his mother's earth.

II

Most of the first day all I had of the world
outside were images. On the second I caught up
with the commentators romping around
on their field day: 'In one sense the Soviet Union
may be witnessing the rebirth of the real
revolution rather than a halfway house
through several false ones.' Gorbachev,
another wrote, underlining the point,
'has enabled 1917 to take up
its proper course again where Lenin had led it
astray.' Everyone was a Revisionist now!
Statues of Lenin were toppling, scythed
at the knees: spinning at the end of a crane,
his famous finger pointed drunkenly
from the Baltic to the Black Sea.

'The rebirth of the real revolution' –
imagine it! In a few words – a pen nib
sleighing through the snow – we were moving
back through History, through the whole
'dustbin of history', or at least seventy-four years
of blood, bone and gristle. Back through the Years
of Stagnation when lives were simply
stifled, imagination throttled at birth; back
through bare dirty rooms in state mental hospitals,
through gulags of hopelessness, the efficiency

and the lies of Kalinin and Babi Yar
and the millions upon millions
of collective killings: above them the faint
nightingale tongues of Pasternak
and Tsvetaeva; and Mandelstam; and Mayakovsky; in times
when, as Akhmatova told it, 'only the dead
smiled, happy in their peace'. And back again
past the cold white campaigns, the bones
crushed beneath all the strident state monuments.
'Forgive me, your president . . .' Till at last
arriving at the small village of Vitebsk,
where the innocent Marc Chagall, newly installed
as commissar for Fine Art, has ordered
posters of giant green cows and flying horses
to float through our imaginations, where lives
his only dream of a perfected world.

'More gas! Gas!' I'd heard your mother shout
and saw her mouth gape like a fish
beneath the mask. Then, surfacing from a dive
down a black rope of pain that seemed to be
crushing the centre of her being, she turned her head
slightly and brushed the midwife's arm
with fingertips to which the blood was just
returning. 'Thank you. You're so kind.'
Nature revealing a truth about her
at that moment as clearly as that day History
had revealed some truth about Yeltsin.
The pain had taken us both by surprise.
'The biggest secret in the world' – so close
to death. 'How long? How long . . . ?' Night
became dawn, became day, became afternoon,
as the forces of nature stormed her,
picked her up, dashed her down. Even before
the worst, in a lull, I looked across
her pale, done-in face and exhausted body
to the midwife. 'It does make you wonder

how when there are so many people in the world
and each of them thrust into the world
in such pain, surely enough to know . . .
enough to value . . .' 'Forgive me,
your president, that I could not . . .'

The day you were born, it was
'A Red Letter Day'. Millions of lives . . .
millions of lives . . . we've wasted.

Oh, my son, your precious, precious head.

Animal

Early morning, the sun
a wheel (if there was one)
on the far horizon
and we in a tall, old
baobab tree, the hot
dung smell of the veldt
rising up to greet us.
In the safe waterhole
below, four buffalo
roll, the gazelles relax
their shivering skins. Squawk!
Birrip-pip-pip! Eek-eek
keek-keek! the old ark
settling its timbers
on the blue open sea.

We three are locked into
stillness, the first mumbling
words several lifetimes
away yet. Our son reaches
a warm arm across one
of your breasts to draw milk

from the earthen stack
of your nipple. My head
resting at the soft edge
of his is a smudging
of skins too far: his paw-
plump hand swipes at me
and a sweet tooth of milk
is lost to the fold
of your breast. Still,
swipe away! my little one

for I'm firm on this tall
old baobab tree,
happy with this branchline
of evolution. Squawk!
Birrip-pip-pip! Lazy preening,
his rinsed blue eyes
between us, a mesh
of arms and thighs, his
finger briefly alighting
on my useless nipple.
So this is innocence,
this measureless moment
when all that concerns us
is the hot shuck of skin
or the casual dismissal
of a fly. But restless
at last he twists between us
and I reach an arm, just,

through the arch of his back
to take him in my arms.
There, gently, I blow and suck,
suck and blow into the soft
creases of his neck.
The animal in him
stills, attentive to the new,

as the warmth spreads until
I am taking as well
as giving succour. Breath!
A trick! Kindling of gods,
source of music, stirring
of these lines: breath breaks
our animal spell.
                    Yet
when the bright morning
finally insists
I leave the safety
of this, our crumpled old
baobab tree, it is with
a snort, a loose-
lipped whinny, that naked
I hunt down my clothes.

Alberta Morning

or How Newness Enters My World

In the limited, aquatic, early-morning light,
so loosely shaped by neat suburban fences

and walls, I lose the edge between what's outside
and in. The looming mass of the freezer, the over-

hanging cupboards, the squat presence
of the cooker with its four wide black eyes; each

seems wild, foreign in its own way, as the broad
body of fir framed by the kitchen window,

its branches snout-thick with filaments
of silvered verdigris, seems halfway

to the domesticity of metal. Yet,
at its highest fleshy point, it's a

timber wolf nosing the striking blue, interceding
between the pure light and the close, dim

interstices of this scene: as the simple pot of cones
you have gathered and placed on the white table

of the deck intercede between the wings
of the fir and barefoot me rooted to this cold floor.

A magpie – one for sorrow – its planed wedge
of a tail perfectly poised, hops across the fading grass,

rhyming with the fence slats. The musty smell
of a full bowl of blueberries beside me billows

into the still air. There is black in the berries.
There is blue in the bird. There is a timber wolf

with blue in the tip of its nose sitting
on top of the fir tree, no not howling, just

staring with my eyes out into the endless blue.
This is how Magritte translates into Albertan

totems; and this is how newness enters my world –
in a simple vocabulary of blue, of fir, of bird

and of berries. Though all along 112th Street
and at all its avenues, the first up look out

on decks and firs and magpies and fences, I hold
this first morning scene – a moment stilled –

as precious, before its power, for me too, is drained
by the commonplace and it is translated

even as the full kettle boils and our child cries,
into the approximations of memory.

Hazards

Cradling a bottle of bittersweet
McNally's, feet up, skimming a *noir* thriller,
a sharp-edged seductress on its cover;

with half an eye I take in game two
of the World Series, the Toronto Blue Jays
(one down) versus the Atlanta Braves.

I've given the aerials a good work out,
yet only in the slo-mo of a curving
pitch or in the real time of a sky-kissed

catch is it clear to me what's going on.
A blurred white trail at the foot of the screen
comes between me and the spicy dialogue.

Freezing rain's made road travel hazardous.
Police warn drivers to keep off the roads.
A moment later, the message repeats.

My wife sits where I'd encouraged her to go,
in the warm embrace of a dark theatre
staring towards the bright lights: her head's tipped

back to secure her glasses, her mind's alive,
generous, but framing questions, possibly
for a coffee house later – a cafe latte

of theatre talk. And all the time
the treacherous world grows more so. Rain welds
into ice where it falls, black roads glint

in moonlight. Cars helplessly collide.
In another room there's another pull.
Our son lies, his plump bottom up in the air,

the soles of his bare feet, two square-
nosed fish on a platter, surrounded
by all the softness we want for his world.

I linger over him in the darkness,
edge him on his side and pull the blankets
over the drowsy question mark he makes:

this, the closest to prayer I get.
We're at the ninth innings when Ed Sprague
takes the ball mid-thigh and devours its heat.

The rest's History. The ball crashes
into an ocean of silenced Braves' fans –
a two run homer, 5 to 4, one game all

and all still to play for. 'I could've crushed
their windpipes one by one and they couldn't
have done a thing to stop me,' sings Easy

also on a roll. *CBC News at Ten*
warns conditions are extremely hazardous
for Croats, Serbs, Bosnians, Somalians,

Tajiks, emigrants, immigrants and Jews.
I sit on the edge of my seat, my beer long
forgotten, waiting for your chopped, cold run

to the door. This is the symmetry of love:
the roots of sympathy growing wider,
deeper, watered by the freezing rains of dread.

Grace

We were the necessary strangers
that Christmas Eve at your parents'
Ukrainian feast. Eyes down, all stood

over the single white candle, a stalk
that burned from a round of plaited bread
as you gave us grace in a language

your childhood tongue never mastered.
Forty-seven, in a loose dress of red red rue,
your mother tactful at your side,

you reached for all the gaping vowels
as a child would, as if your very life
depended on it: *dolia* – fate –

and what fate would you deserve
if you could not save even this short grace
from the oubliettes of history?

So different then from our last goodbyes
when we trailed red prairie dust
in banners all around Two Hills

in search of your summer shack.
In shorts and straw hat, you played,
rather well, the dowager aunt

dismissive of all our excuses
till you bent to blow a smouldering log
to life and soft flakes of blue wood ash

were lost to green poplar tips. Later
we walked to the pond, leaving the vastness
of prairie fields shimmering at our backs.

We were in the landscape now, idling
along its stubbly edges – blowsy poppies,
a darting finch: in some hot agrarian south

of the Old World, closer at last
to the bloodknots of Eastern Europe
you'd spent ten years unravelling.

To fly off the earth (your words) you must
first be standing somewhere: the settled
prairie earth or a darker loam

turned over and over with bones and blood.
There is the gift of bread before us.
As the candle honours and weeps

for it still, you dress the wounds
of an imperfect prayer and send them
like finches, flitting across the abyss.

The Hunt

A final report for Bill Smith (1910–1993),
Iqaluit, formerly Frobisher Bay, Baffin Island, March 1993

'Grief moves from
heart to stapled page
to heart again.'
                    Dale Zieroth

I

Through the whisky haze
of dawn, Frobisher's
Arctic gift drifts
along the royal waters

of the Avon; silently
through the bulrushes
paddle resting
on the kayak top.

A harpoon rises
from a mist of rushes,
a glitter of water
falling from its tip

before it plunges
into a swan's breast
in an outrage of water
and wings.
                    Stillness.

Blood blooming in the water.

From a distance
the virgin queen, whose white
domed forehead's not unlike
a swan's breast, surveys

the chilled faces
which surround her; the soft
cheeks of fish nuzzling the ribs
of a riverbank

as blood billows
over their heads. What she finds
warming in this scene
is its lack of frills:

a swan's neck stretching
in the stubby fist before her;
and an Arctic loneliness
to match her own.

For this, lightly
she traps the damp air
in her ageing hands
again and again.

Of course they rarely hunt like that now, though you can buy tiny
replicas of Inuit in kayaks and other small, rough sculptures of seals,
walrus, narwhal; buy them at the end of a corridor stacked up with the
latest videos. *L. A. Dreams.* Or you can probably buy them wherever
you are, in an elsewhere hungry for what aboriginals can make so that
much of what's made is made without pride – for what's a seal to them
now? The student holds up earrings for the teacher.

> – Are they finished? she asks.
> – You tell me, says the teacher.
> – Well I could sell them, the reply.

There's hunger too, always has been, for stories to fill this vastness,
to give silence a tongue: stories that beyond the edges end, for those
who look from the boat if not for those from the shore, most often in
disappointment, death: both. Take Henry Hudson, explorer, cast adrift
with his son by the *Discovery*'s put upon crew; found by Inuit drifting
dead in James Bay. Their testimony:

Hudson's son
their first white boy
they tie up
in a dog harness –
for what use can he be? –
and stake outside their tent.
His fingers are already
useless, his fists
paws as he keeps the huskies
at bay
before their noses go down
for the night. And here
the real fight begins
to eke out strength
from a scatter of seal bones
and frozen marrow.
          For tomorrow
blinded by Arctic light
he pulls for his life
through pack ice green
as apples. His sinews are tough
as a bear's though ridge
upon ridge of ice knives
his bloodied paws. Still
at the day's end
they love him for it,
allow him to nuzzle
their fishy crotches
as once he had his mother's
velvet gown. Now
he's their favourite dog for sure
petted in igloo warmth, loved
back into language,
into the human world
once more. But first
tonight
he must endure

the howls of grief
the doggy whimpers
of a child
at his comfortless fate.
His loneliness is ready
to match it when the big moon
rises over the ice
and he stiffens
to a perfect white.

Sure the North's more
than stories. But I'm casting around
all the time, Bill. This is your trip too
and I'm trying to find a story for you. Here's one
at least to make you smile.

In Inuktitut, Iqaluit means *fish*. But if you spell it beginning I-Q-U it
means *arsehole*. It's not that, yet it still has the portacabin feel of the
place most of which the US Air Force threw up in '42: provisional,
sitting on the ice, no purchase on the land – except at night when the
random spray of lights gives it that intimate feel of places built before
the car. An irony to remind you of North African evenings from the
Arctic! And not true of course, though at times I only recognise roads
when skidoos come hurtling down them. But then they go everywhere,
ubiquitous as children on slides or the giant ravens which croak as if
this were a sanctuary built only for them.

So look around. Where's History?
What constitutes achievement?
Ask Franklin. (Now that
is a good story.)

And once all your stories
have been taken from you . . .

Who do you fear children?

Drunk men. Dogs.

II

Another three fingers, Bill.

We're casting off
heading north again, further
than either of us
has ever been or one
will go again. Could be
we're only making tracks
to silence
            but tell you
what I'm after –

There has to be a poem
after the poem
at last finding
its place in the heart;
not funnelled
into a form as if
its song could be
contained, its grief
assuaged, merely
through its telling.
We'd know then
the grief
on the stapled page
would be a lie
fixed there
out of its true
habitat
where the strong
milky light
gives it colour,
the cold air feeds it.
No. The poem
after the poem,
the poem we're

heading towards
always, is the only
true poem, free
as a cliff of fulmar
to change shape,
to roost, to be forgotten,
to be silent; like the Arctic tern
to disappear in icy wastes
or there to be
augmented. So

6 a.m. and four of us up
and off to a caribou hunt.

III

We skirt the town and its graveyard of simple white crosses. Pack ice
glows pink, green, in the early morning light. Derek the hunter on lead
skidoo zigzags across the gulley to get the lie of the land, then strikes out
for the white nowhere. We ride along the top of a ridge, the top of the
world, a lie that holds to the last moment when abruptly we're folded
onto another one and another and another. I bounce on my skidoo,
scream delight through my frozen balaclava, though at the same time
feel I could let my head droop onto the handlebars, fall into the deepest
of woolly sleeps.

We spot a frieze of caribou grazing snow over yet another rise – a herd
of about a dozen a quarter of a mile away. Derek takes his rifle from its
scabbard, climbs a rocky escarpment. A hollow thud without echo and a
caribou drops while others scatter. The wounded caribou rises. Falls to its
knees. The herd's confused, directionless. *Die, please die,* Leigh mutters.
Derek on foot moves closer. I hold hunter and hunted in my gaze as he
raises his rifle through a light glitter of snow. Then it's over and he's walk-
ing purposefully towards his kill. The only moving thing in all I see.

When we arrive on the skidoos the caribou, a female, is still twitch-
ing, a smear of blood from her stomach dripping onto the snow. *Just
nerves,* Derek says. *She's dead,* passing an ungloved hand over her startled
brown eyes and nostrils. But he jabs his short knife deep into her neck
to make sure.

To work! She must be skinned and butchered before she freezes. He runs his knife up the inside of her legs, peels them; turns her onto her back; slits her arse to throat. Thrusting his hands deep into her warmth he eases the pepper and white hide down from the stomach and its crimson contents well out. At least he has missed the bladder where the Inuit believe the soul is seated. Skinned now, he hacks off the bony forelegs and tosses them into a pile of waste (on one hoof a trail of blood frozen dark as tar). *For the foxes*, he says. Into another pile, to be wrapped in the fresh skin and put in the sled, go the haunches, the strips of back, rump etc.

Her innards, an intricately beautiful world of marble and root, pour out onto the bloodied snow. A foetus swells there: a kidney-shaped smoothness a couple of months from birth, it's a wonder her slight body could contain it. *Ah, we're making her smaller now*, says Derek in his Newfoundland-Irish accent. *No, it's no sport this*, he says, stabbing at the neck to sever the head. *Here, stamp on these somebody*; he indicates the ribs with knife and fist the blood have almost made one. *Come on Derek,* I say, *let's see the foetus. We've seen everything else.*

Holding the haft loosely at its end, he swings the blade lightly through the sack and the amniotic fluid gushes out dampening the snow. He flicks the head out with the tip of his knife; the lilac body slithers after. Vegetable still, the ears are folded leaves, flat against the doglike head; soft hooves pointed like a bunch of purple iris heads, stems no thicker than the umbilical cord. We take this in in silence till Derek, who's been rubbing his hands with snow, says, *Oh I almost forgot – the tongue.* He picks the head up by a horn, slits the throat up-a-ways, lifts the tongue out and slices it off at root. *That one hurt,* says Leigh.

But there's something about the speed
with which the caribou becomes
food for us and food for foxes, the sureness
of Derek's touch in all he does –
even to the remembering
of that long tongue lolling from his fist –
that gives him a place on this blank page
below the clear blue sky: and that speaks,
strange though it may sound, Bill,
of love.

The rest of us trap hot mugs of tea
in our hands; not a breath of wind
yet the cold stiffens us. Raising our mugs
we drink to the power
of his transforming art.

IV

I paw the ground
round the churned site
of the kill; rouse
below the thin snow crust
the raw smell
of earth, soon to be
graced with its carpet
of purple saxifrage,
buttoned by snow-white avens.
Raising my head
I sniff
the air, the light; angle
an ear towards
silence.

     Beyond
the next silvery
blue ridge I sense
there's nothing
to hold me; though death
remains
historical, certified,
here on this stapled page,
love and memory
gather up the remains
where they lie
for all to find them
and tell
another story
in which the swan flies
over my head, the Inuit

comes home, the caribou
calves to the young boy's
delight; and you
brush that glitter of snow
from your shoulders
before the whisky's poured,
the tongue's loosened
and the story
begins.

Jenny in July

rolls off the mat, escapes
into the shade of a thicket
of broom. Grass feels

cool on bare arms
and legs, as her hands, still
clumsy as paws, swim

through tall stems, almost
bring heavy seed-heads
to her milky lips. She'll learn.

For now, she's the most
defenceless of all summer's
creatures, abandoned

on a green doorstep
by a father who'd once
dreamed of his daughter

brushed by a fistful
of herbs, rolled in pastry
light as air, cooked

in the wink of an eye.
None of it had bothered
her at all – or him – the dish

was simply a thought –
how tender! how sweet!
Now the yellow stitches

of nipplewort shine
over her, always out of reach,
as she kicks herself ever

further into the world
of flowers and of foxes
along her rich river-bed.

The Father

Our son breaks our sleep
with unconscious screaming: I don't
want to. I don't want to. I don't . . .

Want raspberry? Strawberry? This book
or that? So few real choices
he has in his life. I decide

to keep a small bag packed
for us both. When the time comes
I'll be ready. Sure enough

one evening, able to take no more
of our feeding patterns, he's off.
He's stronger than I thought

and more determined. In no time
we've cleared the last houses
and are in open country where

the whispering barley's ripe
for plucking; swifts dart in
shallow loops over our heads.

For some time we drift south,
taking lifts if we're offered
or looping back on our trail.

He's definitely getting used to
calling the shots: so some days
we'll be lions all day till my palms

ache; others spend by the roadside
piling stones till each cairn
casts its own tiny shadow

across his busy fists.
What we'll do when the money
runs out I haven't yet figured

but the nights grow warmer
and I find we need less and less.
Perhaps it seems strange to give

your life over to the whims
of a child, to spend it always
in the hinterland. Who can say

how it will work out or what
lessons, if any, we're learning?
Down among the blowsy poppies,

I disturb a wild bee
gorging at a daisy's heart.
It kicks out a yolkyellow leg

and I see him at his mother's
breast again, and think of
the distances we've travelled.

from *Landscapes and Legacies*
(2003)

Hoboes

Europe, between wars

'I got stones in my passageway
and my road is dark as night'
                    Robert Johnson

I

Brother, here lives a kind woman –

Chance brought me to her door.
She took me in without question
filthy as I was. How long

had I been dancing? Hard to tell.
I came to myself, yelping like a dog
round a sycamore. She called me

from the shadows, her cats' milk
dripping from my chin. Cats,
the kindest keep them. She'd two,

black as night. They wove
between her ankles; they came
to me as she bathed and bound

my bleeding feet. Kindness, hatred –
who's closer to the Mysteries
than we are? – the look of one, the brush

of the other. She lived alone
with an orphaned busy-ness
even my needs couldn't touch.

I saw her eyes, in passing, kiss
the mantel portrait of a waxen soldier
more than once. I took to the barn

with a blanket from her bed,
bread and cheese from her table.
Through a crack in the wood

I saw the moon – the first time
in a long time – as a possible friend.
And that night, I swam without pause

from one empty room to another.
I woke with a knocking at her door,
then the rough, insistent voices.

II

Brother, you should have heard me!

At first, I gleaned our old familiar,
Suspicion, from her eyes. It was
the children brought me to her –

I'd taught them pick-up-sticks
in the lane. *Wait there* – they'd bring me
tea with sugar, milk; bread and jam.

All the while, their bright eyes flitted
between us. Look! – we've brought
a maimed bird to your door.

There were three of them, lithe
as cats, and briefly trusting too.
As one handed me the bread

I told how happy I'd been up north:
good job . . . lovely wife . . . O every
possible blessing, till a story

of sudden betrayal lifted me
out of my life, clear of
the growing of my children, to live

on the road, keeping secret shrines,
a guardian of only my own ageing.
It was a toss up: that one

or the Jesus story, and I chose well
for without further word she brought
thick slices of pork, a blanket

of good grey wool. Yet even
in triumph, wreathed in her smile,
I couldn't shake the loss of what

I'd never had. Brother, beware
the power of your own persuasions.
                                        At times
better an empty belly, the open road.

III

Brother, when she laid eyes on me,

she called him double quick; the pair of them
side by side, filling out the doorway.
Whatever they said, I had their meaning.

What do you want?
You can't stay here. You must leave.
Leave now. Their eyes, jittery

as caged birds, scanned the horizon:
what lay beyond the roads that brought me
to their door? 'We're good people,'

she told me, thumbs buried in her fists. 'But . . .'
I stood – call this the Third Art –
letting her words fall into silence.

A child poked a blunt head round her legs.
I smiled at the child. 'Please,' its mother said.
Brother, the first two arts will save your bacon,

but only if you're quick. The Third Art
is to trust in stillness. St Francis
had it in spades. All other holy men too.

In the end, she'd no answer
to whatever brought the thumping
to her chest. Round the back,

sun on a sweet-smelling wood stack,
he slopped milk into my tin mug;
she pushed at me half a loaf of fruit bread.

'Now,' he said, near to being friendly,
'head for the birch wood. It's dense. I work
the fields close by. More of your kind's

hiding out in there. I've heard pipes,
seen the shadows dancing.'
His 'good luck' barely reached my back.

I took it for someone else's prayer.

IV

Brother, this is a good place to be.

The couple are old, the house
and the dogs sleep early. Time then
to leave the barn, *To walk out*

of an evening. My advice, head
for the orchard; even in clearest
moonlight, its trees will hide you.

You'll stroll between their slim
and eager young branches, plucking
an apple here, a plum or two there.

It's like living in the strange land
of Plenty. You may choose to eat
as you pick; at other times

collect a lap full of fruit
and lie against a tree, breathing in
the rising sweetness. How can you

know anticipation when you
have nothing? It's only
to invite a fanged beast to your door.

But now, the fruit
gathered, let the moment last
as long as you want it to. This

is the beginning of things again –
a church of earth and of air. Let
the darkening world beyond

this sleepy farm fend for itself –
moonlight and fruit are yours.
But brother, don't stay too long,

be careful where you pick –
a pattern of bark-wounds
can be read clear as any book.

Contained appetites are better
for those who return; those
lucky enough to come after.

V

Brother, didn't you read the signs?

This is no place to linger. Once
we were shadows, seasonal as plants.
But, though their eyes kept us

at the furthest rim of vision, crouching
in half light over our tidy fires,
not much missed us

of the silhouettes that fought
or danced in lamplight; we heard
the kicked dog yelp, the low moan

of the rotten-hoofed beast;
the snagged sheep calling out
to an indifferent flock.

Of course when she was found,
on a bed of crushed anemones,
her white chest naked as a swan's,

they preferred to think evil
had been imported: that the theft
of a few hen's eggs or a slack udder

were preludes to such a cruelty.
He laid her down, the cord beside her,
and scrabbled around in wood litter.

He glanced my way, then
sniffed the air. I tell you he knew
someone was watching. But what's

our word worth? Stay –
they'll get us both for something.
Over the border, so I've been told's

a safe place to camp and fresh water.
See that broken old stump on the skyline?
From there, you're on your own.

VI

Sister? I've heard the stories too –

the clear shape of you curled
in morning mist, cut
from the evenings' shadows. What was it

drove you onto the road, to live like this –
no home, no love, only these coded
messages, these random notes to ourselves?

It's said, most often, you pass
as a man with a heavy coat,
a scarf, worn like a cowl, nodding

resolutely as if no force
could face you. But beneath the coat,
so say those who've caught you

in river or lake, the uncoiled nest
of hair a shadow-you swimming
beside you, your nakedness

is only one of many signs. Is it
you then that unites us? You
who moves between us in our

orphanhood, making us feel –
who are careful to feel – we may not be
so completely alone. Sister –

when I pass by a blue shrine
I imagine it is you. When I am a dog
burrowing in the damp earth, I smell

the first effulgence of spring
and imagine it is you. When I feel
the slight wind on my brow at night

I imagine your fingers, your lips,
passing onto me the sweetness
of a mother, a lover, a daughter, a wife.

VII

Brother, there are times in sleep

I'm in a world that's fresh
with new signs; birds I feel
I know yet can't quite name.

I'm at home there, sunning myself
on top of a freight car beneath a sky
that scrolls out blue and blue

and blue over an endless prairie.
By the time I reach one coast
I'm forgotten at the other. I pass

over the earth just once. At times
I meet others of my kind – men
and women rich in stories. We fish a river,

fiercely blue as the sky; cook trout
over an open fire, sing sad songs
we wouldn't have any other way.

I got stones in my passageway
and my road is dark as night.
It is better is it not than living

in this world of black and white,
cleaving to a rail track as thick smoke
shrouds us where we crouch

in the shadows? When I go round
the doors with my clothes pegs
or a basket of whittled dolls

I've to get a story out quick –
and a strong one too! – or I'm fucked
by a fable I can't escape. In their dreams

I'm bound in black rags: some kind
of carrion poisoning water wells,
picking over their dead.

VIII

Brother, how I got here's a mystery:

sleeves like washing on a line
drew me; washing that moved
to a musical line, say the droned

exhalation of a bagpipe. The shirts hung
from a hand cart or a trailer;
and a straggle of men followed

after the cart, singing softly
as if to themselves,
'More light! More light!'

The shirts were for hire –
woollen they were, the colour
of straw. We wore them loose

over our clothes and tied
a thick worsted tie round our necks
like a noose. So dressed

we followed the trailer or cart
and smiled on our fellow men
as we shuffled along like pilgrims –

yes, pilgrims is what we seemed to be.
And though the light was strong,
and stronger yet as the day wore on,

still we sang, 'More light! More light!'
It wasn't a musical – it felt so real!
And if it was a dream,

then other bloods had lived it.
As our shirts bathed in the burning
fields of light, it was unclear

whether we were celebrating
or mourning; chanting in elegy
for the darkness we were leaving

or in praise of the open road ahead.

Crabs: Tiree

We tied a worm of bacon fat
to a flat rock with string
and dropped it over the edge
into the clear water
of the bay. It fell gently

to the sand and the seaweed.
A tug told us we'd a bite
or we saw the crab itself
latch onto the ragged fat and pulled it
steadily out: this was the knack.

Too sudden, too sharp
and it dropped from its stone
shadow, so clumsily evading
its fate. But smoothly
feeding the rough string

through fist upon fist
and they would come to us
like lumps of lava, water
sluicing from their backs.
Dumbly determined

they hung on
by one improbable claw
before the dull crack as they hit
the harbour wall or the side
of the pails we kept them in.

Standing in a row
four or five of us holiday kids
pulled out scores in a day till each
bucket was a brackish mass
of fearsome crockery

bubbling below
its skin of salt water.
What happened to them all? –
our train of buckets, the great stench
of our summer sport.

It was a blond boy
from Glasgow finally pushed me in
head over heels from where
I crouched on the pier wall.
When I righted myself

I was waist deep in crab-
infested waters. No one
could pull me out. 'You must walk
to the shore,' my sister shouted
as I held my hands

high above my head
thinking I could at least
save them. But how beautiful
it was all around me! The spatter
of green crofts

and deep blue lochans,
the cottontail, the buttercup
on the cropped foreshore. The sky
was depthless; all was silence.
And I was there

moving slowly through
this perfect blue wedge
bearing terror in one hand, guilt
in the other, leaving the briefest wake
to mark my shame.

Mr McArthur

The rogue sheep on its knees nudges
a bony head at the kettle
of milk on my lap. I hold both
handle and lid with canny conceit,
for the kettle's tin sides
are in the broad grip of our host
Mr McArthur himself whose arm
brushes my cheek with sweet
smells of straw and milk.
                              Each evening
he places the white jug of milk
straight from the cow beside butter
and jam. And for a moment
stands in the door, a large-boned florid
featured man whose bottom teeth jut
over toothless gums. Our mother smiles
with a 'That-will-be-fine-thank-you,'
and a shoulder-straightening that says
No childish words please – on the still
steaming milk its surface jewelled
with golden gobs of fat.
                              The oiled coat
of the sheep brushes my knees
and I curl my fingers away
from the desperate milk-whiskered mouth.
What a useless little bugger
I am! Seven years old I let slip
two faded floral cups, then
watch Mr McArthur bearing
the pieces away like petals
in his raw hands. A gate's spar cracks
when I swing on it; a door's slat –
I swear – caves in before the wind.
But Mr McArthur simply
smiles or tuts as if nothing

is worth anything – or as if
the landscape of wind, rain and sea
is too fluid for the tight space
of apology we'd pen him in.

Saying goodbye in that boxed hall
with the new-mended door, I sense
the generous presence of his life;
the routine acts he's opened up
to me. How have I repaid him?
We have no language but this
clumsy disclosing of ourselves.
My tears are black on the stone flags.
I know they are no apology
but in the stiff silence *sorry's*
not what I want to say most.

Clestrain: Orkney

Boyhood home of John Rae, Arctic explorer

On a cloud-stacked spring afternoon
you can hear how even the mildest wind
buffets your voice into a mourn-
ful staccato, how words are thinned

down to their roots. Yet his voice
rasped through the elements, on the edge
of each curt order, a savage
delight in hardship. At the *noust* –

the cleft of rock where his sailboat
was once snug – I turn from the shore
and, cleaving to a dyke for shelter,
take the track to the sensibly squat

house of Clestrain. Here the wind's cut
and the stones tell only of absence,
broken by a last pigeon caught
fluttering out one more vacant lens.

There's a skeleton grandeur still –
the curled ironwork that lurches
from the staircase – a dainty school
indeed for the man who marched

till his moccasins were blood-shod;
who made soup from rotting fish-bones
and claimed you knew nothing of food
till you'd drained the last juices down

from a ptarmigan's toes. The thoughts
spool on, with a creak from a board,
a scuffed stone; a vision that rots
in the silence: the place can't hoard

the man. Out in the minch, a boy
hauls on a flapping sail, careless
of weather. Rain shushes like a sleigh;
flinty waves strain in their tresses.

But the boy looks past the cloth he holds
to the horizon's sudden silver:
beyond which lies death – or adventure –
and over which the stories roll.

Strawberries

The Algonquins, Canada

In the middle of a landscape
that could lose us – one small boat
and a sun jigsawing away
great bays of black waters to give

one last rhythmic shape of light –
Rosa's hand uncups a harvest
of wild strawberries she's gathered
on the lake's shore. In muted light,

each red fleck glows: a tiny coal,
the whole a brazier of strawberries,
which calls from us all something brief
but shared – delight or prayer –

before we press out their sweetness
with our tongues. A dragonfly
comes at us now from far along
its steady thread of flight. In fact,

we're losing detail fast – the lake's
brimming to a darkening crush
of firs, appears to be a step higher
than us. This boat's heading

for the impossible, I think,
as one heron, then another,
heave themselves from the shadows and,
trailing the grainy daylight, take

all the time two blue herons need
to sew darkness onto darkness
across the bay. Any time now,
the riper stars will start to glow.

By the time we're barbecuing
back at base, our hungry eyes'll
scoop them up like beer nuts, rootless
and rife in every patch of sky.

The Gift

from Andy Goldsworthy

I thought, given they were small
as children's fists, the pigeon's breasts
would cook quickly. But my wife

found them too rare. She pointed out
at the end of one clean pink slit
the bloody hole the shot had made.

Blood eased onto my white plate too
and I thought then of what we'd said
before your gift of the liquid

bag of breasts. In your new workshop
a snowball of deer blood had melted
onto a stretch of paper. The blood

was vermilion, shockingly *there*.
We shared a recall of the Arctic,
of caribou butchered on snow.

That blood on the fresh snow,
how beautiful it was and how
the hunters' artistry gave us

our memories intact. Blood. Mud.
Every day working with what you find –
your sketch books too, drawn in mud.

Fitting then to find here a ghost
of Rembrandt's rack of beef, even
Chardin's eviscerated skate.

And, for me, to contemplate words
and the silence they're pulled from –
and how they end up on the plate.

Caravaggio in Dumfries

On the first ever day of spring, Caravaggio
strolls over the old stone bridge to market.

There, he orders three pounds of pippins,
two of red delicious, one each of bananas

and of pears. His eye tells him what's ripe,
what's sweet, crisp or tart. Lastly, he points

to a large bunch of inky-blue grapes. *Per favore.*
'Nice ones these,' remarks the vendor –

a tiny lady in a black Bulls cap with one
winking gold tooth. She's noticed how

taken her customer is with the grapes.
Caravaggio thinks he'll paint them later,

include them in his knowing *Little Bacchus* –
that sallow-skinned portrait of his self.

He is twenty or so – fresh from the country –
and what he feels this warming morning

standing before these piled fruit stalls
is not innocence but wide-eyed appetite –

an openness to all fecundity. History
will call him *stormy petrel*, tempestuous,

libidinous; temper as much as fever
will eventually kill him. But this morning

all that feels so unlikely; impossible even,
as he heads for home, cradling his five bags of fruit.

At the bridge head, one of a pair of swans,
circling its young, raises itself from the river

and lifts up its wings. A slab of white light
hits Caravaggio with a shock of pleasure

like a lover's open thigh, a magnificence
that folds in on itself, as indeed light folds

into darkness. A lesson his eye takes in
before he returns across the sparkling waters.

Simon in the Vegetable Patch

At the end of rows of runner beans
(perfect, proud, erect) your peas,
equally perfect and sweet as I remember –

a taste in tact from childhood –
lie in a tangle of their own devising.
With a bundle of canes like pick-up-sticks,

a ball of twine, a knife as red
as a rooster's comb whose blade
winks in the sun, you spend an afternoon

half-hour; no real notion
what you're doing, only what you want
to achieve – to bring those peas to order!

You think in planes, in angles,
in zigs and zags: a stage set for peas
to shine like blades, to lift themselves

onto open palms. Somehow it's disaster.
But at least it's half an hour
when not much else is happening.

Your daughter tops a white cap
with sunshine; her eyes the centre
of all that is; a picture that spirals

beyond her mother, her mother's friends,
the busy hens, the pony that stands,
head bowed in private penance;

out yet to green maps of alder and ash
that ripple with health till the blue sky
clips them. But at last, hey ho,

a solution. Your blade rides
through knotted twine; you amass
an airy pile of branches – 'something

more . . . *informal,*' you say. Too late!
The company calls on you – a walk
to the grey, roiling sea. And sweetly

you accept, though there'll be nothing to show
for this half hour of all your labours –
as there's nothing to show

for half an hour when your daughter
sat in the sun and smiled and laughed
at her mother, her mother's friends,

the busy hens, the penitent pony,
and the ash, the alder, the rows
of runner beans and peas where her father

worked carefully, without care,
puzzling over a tiny piece of green chaos
while there was order everywhere.

Mushrooms

West Cork, Ireland

Today in the lee of the islands of Sherkin,
Castle, Calf, Clear and Hare, the small island
of Skeam East turns like a ragged butterfly
in a blue, wingless sea. Roaring Water Bay

can never have seemed so inaptly named.
In the fields above the island ruins, Dan and I,
the sun on our shirtless backs, pick mushrooms
in an idly purposeful way. They're everywhere,

extended families of milky white heads
shining in the summer's still cropped green.
And the houses, I ask – a scatter of stone husks
above the landside bay – when were they

abandoned? Hard to say: famine some; others
as late as the fifties. A hundred years or so
of a drifting death. I'm pulled to the island's
furthest edge, fooled by a handful of bone-

white crab shells. Water slaps into beaker-
smooth gulleys. An open boat chugs past, the dull
plops of lobster pots measuring the silence.
Together we fill a bucket with mushrooms

and cache them in a mesh of broken ferns;
then go off in search for more, strolling
aimfully through the open fields, leaving few
for those who'll come after. 'Stuff 'em!'

I agree. Later as our families trail back
across the spit of land to where Dan's boat
tugs at the slightly less sandy beach, I idle
in a ruin, crouching below the rafters'

stone slots. The small windows have turned
from the landscape around them. Like a vegetable
beneath a box bed, I am brushed by the spores
of a shadow life the light can't touch.

That night our cornucopia of mushrooms
boils down into a mess of slippery ashes,
into the salty, blue-black ink of themselves.
Their juices colour everything they touch

with a fisherman's dye. It's the colour
of cold hearths, of a louring sky, of the grit
at the sea's edge after the storm has passed
and the Wreckers' eyes shine in the darkness.

Island Love

You walk up from the strand, your creel brimming
with herring; you come down from the hill,
your creel laden with turf, your grey-green eyes
cast down on the stony path, your black hair

wet with sweat or a moil of salty mist;
and glad am I there's a bond between us
for it seems to me I'm a poor catch
for this world. My fishing lines tangle and break

in calm waters, lobsters climb from my pots
to go seeking greater challenge elsewhere;
when the sea heaves and gurls black, I'm the first
to lose hope. I set sail with hymns on my lips.

Others there are that would have built for you
a better house; stones that knitted tightly
against the bitter wind, capped with a roof
the hens couldn't lay in. Such men would have turf

stacked for ten winters and then turf to spare;
men to make you proud their knowledge was sought,
their courage praised: for did they not leap
Bull's Cove for you, from black rock to black rock,

as down below fulmars wheeled and the white
water thundered in? They did? God bless them!
But you have a dreamer, a grim fisher
in melancholy; an idler who stares

into the tell-tale smoor of the fire, his tale
often the heaviest creel you carry.
Feckless, your father called me, *indolent*,
your mother: our tongue is rich in name-tags.

Your love is a mystery and a blessing.
No matter where the black dogs take me,
towards overhang or scree, you guide me
back to clear tracks of sunlight; constantly

living our lives the shape of the journey
they are on. You make plans for the market
and provision for each birth. You let faith
take care of the rest – a deep faith that shines

in those bright grey-green eyes, a faith that sees
the lines of my life when I do not,
that welcomes me dripping from the dark sea
when we give up our tired white bodies with joy.

At La Poivière

At La Poivière, the old words come to me –
the soft plosives of *bower* and *bough* –
as I stand below a fiery vault
of cherries. In the filtered sunshine,
first I hold the ladder for my son
as he reaches up to another bright cluster
and drops them in the bowl. And as he does,
so I reach out from the heart of the tree
and feed on those perfect little planets,
coldly burning, which orbit his ankles.

But you're clamouring for your chance too
to harvest plenty, to pluck a treasure
so willing it makes us needlessly laugh.
Soon, your industry's sending our son
running for 'Something! Anything!' Nothing
will stop you now, as you toss down
handfuls for me to hold for the coming bowl.
Only I don't. Part-hidden from you
by one of those leafy boughs, I slip
the cherries, one by one, into my mouth.

With tongue and teeth, I ease out the stone
and the sweet flesh is gone by the time
I spit the pit into the dry earth
or at the crumpled green handkerchiefs
of lettuce. You will, after all, pick more
than my hand or a bowl will bear.
And when you do, I'll reach out again
around your skirts to harvest whatever
falls within my reach; thinking, somewhere here
is a parable concerned with love or beauty.

Rainy Day Mayenne

Rain falls on the brindled cows
composed within their loose pen of poplars;

on the empty duck pond with its square,
flat-bottomed boat. While quadrilles of chestnuts

and limes shoulder the storm, you
blow soap bubbles into the sherry-dark.

Sizeable fruits they are, each one at least
an apple, though now and again, a sweet

little cantaloupe, almost waisted, falls
from your hooped lips. We marvel

at your steady puckered breath; at the soft
watery explosions, the meaningless

blessings we reach for with our open palms –
'let it come! *let it come!'*– as outside rain falls

on the lonely old roads, on churches spaced
like stations – see, in each, St Joan rising

cleanly from flaming tracks. And rain falls
on the war memorials, each name a prayer –

never again – and on the villages
where geraniums disburse their brilliant mould

round windows, doors and walls. I love you
unencumbered like this –

lost in what you do.
                    Outside a buzzard,
carved from a fence post, takes off

in the drizzle and looks down on a landscape
held by the seams of Roman roads

and by the ramparts of chestnuts and limes,
now shimmering in a rain-stopping light.

On Hearing of Your Illness

So how did it happen? Twenty-five years
of friendship – not one minute of it
on foreign soil (and no love letter
till this). The closest we came, the past

glorious summer in the west. We lived it
without doors at Ravenstone, surrounded
by sycamore and beech so richly green
not a breath of wind touched us; the corn

ripened at our backs beneath a sun
that made each day its predicate. We drove
one afternoon to a beach on the Mull,
down hot little roads slashed by sunlight

and shadows, to find a white eiderdown
of mist had rolled over the Irish Sea.
I picnicked in the moony sun, digging
my heels into the sand, while I watched you

wade into the mist, poised as if you bore
a clay pot on your head through heat and dust;
and emerge from it too as if time hadn't
touched you in all those years, your body

a companion piece to your teenage son's.
You waved then to a world composing itself
in those brown otter-bright eyes. That summer
anyone with a boat pulled mackerel

from the glassy bay. Freezers were stacked
with them, yet each day brought fresh offers.
On my last night at Ravenstone, we cooked
the petrol-shiny fish on a wood fire,

the flesh so white, so fresh, it fairly crumbled
in your hands. We shared a grassy mound,
a rowdy crowd of renegades, our air
suffused with sweet smells of woodsmoke

and marijuana. It was, let's say,
Wigtownshire exotic! Some months later,
I heard of the phosphorus bombs raked
from Beaufort's Dyke: 4,000 fire-sticks,

caked with decades of rust that littered
these pilgrim shores. And I recalled a slight
unsteadiness as you'd waved from the sea's edge,
before that clouded landscape took you to its heart.

Pilgrim

When you arrive at the White Loch of Myrton,
that's not the end of your journey, though
for the time you are there it may seem so.

For the White Loch will say, Lay it down –
why don't you? – the tired old rhetoric of self.
Contradiction, sophistry, hope or regret –

shove it all overboard like a lump
of machinery that's never quite made sense;
that's simply been something for you to work on.

Even now as it slips behind the scene,
the one you've called, 'White Loch of Myrton',
you feel how its arcane circuits absorb you.

But *you* are something altogether different,
sitting on a smooth rock-stool by the water's edge,
as so-slow bees drone between buttery blobs

of ragwort and trout click their watery tongues
whenever your back is turned. You are not
the heavy load you've cast aside. You share

instead something of the deep unruffled
stillness of the water, the bluish haze
of bulrushes, the load line between the trees

and their reflections. Hold to that lightness
and see how easy it is to love at the White
Loch of Myrton, where you have no history

but this moment. Still you'd be a fool
if you thought the White Swan of Myrton
would find any of this lovable in you.

And you were a fool to think you could love her.
Tending three dowdy chicks almost as big
as herself, she spits into your reverie:

Go refreshed, she says, but remember,
pilgrim, you cannot live forever on the edge
of the White Loch of Myrton.

from Landscapes

'There is a time in life when you just take a walk:
And you walk into your own landscape.'
from Sketchbook 1, Willem de Kooning (1904–1997)

1

Dense rhododendron bushes almost mask
the start of the track. Oak boughs cast

shadows on sunlit days across it. Ferns
grow unchecked. Once milk churns

and linen passed by to the Big House
and, halfway along, a walled garden still shows

raspberries like spinning tops. The iron door
lies open. Within these walls, desire

rises in you like sap. The world pounds
with green fire: *find me*, you pray, *find me*.

5

The lilac drops, so full in the dusk,
you let it brush your lips, let it mask

the face you give only to evening;
to laurel, dark as an old engraving

of rain. Out of its thick hatching, the bright
orange light of a blackbird's beak

draws you on. To follow its rhythms
is to fill your mouth with a song of earth:

as night falls, to see the distant hills dusted
with a purple that's closer to rust.

8

Who was your father died a long time ago
and now lies through the programmed doors

lit like a hologram – a landscape
of the mind; though his eyelids are mapped

with blue ink and shaving nicks still glower
with crumbs of blood. You want to ease down the nap

of his dry lips but, when you stoop, fear
you'll pass right through his body's thick flow

of light. Instead, you stub your lips on a head
smooth and cold as a tide-washed stone.

9

Each of us is born on an open field,
yet we die in a forest.
                    Polish proverb

One with a nondescript but muddy track,
somewhere on the border of an eastern bloc

whose ill-paid guards have long absconded.
One in whose deep, boggy reaches, wounded

but shapely as tongues, boats have surfaced.
The low croon of ancient voices is laced

through the trees. One, as children, we wandered
into. In the fir-mirk, you tag your father,

his cap on backwards, whooping between trees,
running ever further into darkness.

14

The lights are all out. The wind passes
whispering by you, leaving traces

of voices you will not hear again.
It's summer by the light of your moon:

sand dunes cast shadows like perfect fans.
So what did you lose on that beach? Whose hand,

cold as the North Sea, wakes you tonight?
Let it go, let it go. Let me be a noust

for you. A curse on that landscape's bitter cry.
The lights are all out. The wind passes me by.

15

The empty bell. The dead birds in the house
beat in your breast. Whatever's upset them,

the coming storm, a call they cannot answer,
the peace you thought you'd bought for them – a truce

that's now been broken – you feel their wings rise
against your heartbeat, their small bones swerve

and swerve again, feathering their dying panic.
Deep, in the small black rocks

of their eyes, are windows onto fields and sky –
and the darker rocks against which their wings tire and break.

16

No spring this evening. No fruits under the leaves.
James Wright's line, *I have wasted my life,*

plays through your mind. The river is flooded,
but one bridge seems as good as another

to watch the thick braids of muddy water,
the broken trunk, the tyre the youngbloods

drive down to see. You shuffle through other nights,
other landscapes, but can't re-make the map

that led to this cold balustrade
along lineaments of fiction and of hope.

17

The lamp is a heart, emptying itself
across your desk. If you've any wealth

you'll find traces of it here: the bright cheeks
of worthless objects, fruits from withered stalks.

Your friend, the adventurer's sailed away.
(Pieces of driftwood, tokens, history.)

In all things weighty, he worries he's light.
But you'll write him a letter. You'll post it tonight.

Over the clear white paper on your desk,
the heart is a lamp, emptying itself.

18

Fionnghal sails home from Carolina.
Contact with death's turned her from minor

actress into something much darker.
Tears like Finnan haddies hang from her;

each marks a son lost in a wildwood war,
far from this hold with its foul beds of heather.

She knows now that dandy's accent made no sense –
a landscape at odds with its audience –

and wonders how her own travels will sound
once her vowels open up back on home ground.

19

When you drink water, think about the source,
the Chinese say. One reason to travel.

So, with the proper dispensations,
and a new breed of horse – hot-blooded, large-

lunged – we fought through thunder, lightning and hail
to reach the Heartland. Each night wolves

attacked our camp. Eagles tracked us. All the way
to a marshy field, a non-place; a barren core.

Enlightened, I took note: *The source is where*
                           the river's not there anymore.

20

You tell me there's a path if I simply look.
But the clearest route to it's blocked

with black, boggy mud; pools so dark
and inert, insects score them like pencil marks.

How do I trust those spongy stacks of turf?
If one gives, will I have enough

spring in my step to make the next uncertainty?
And the path itself advances with such shy

hopes up the mountain – a mere trickle of sand –
only to find clouds drowned in a blue tarn.

22

Nothing they found clad darkness better than stone.
In such darkness only they felt safe and warm,

for then it was theirs to control. Our days
are spent touring such spots: the gentle rise

of homes and tombs, like beehives opened
up to light. On the beach, we too blend

smooth stones in a ritual of play which
somewhere goes beyond that into a rich

imagining. At night I rise above a nest
covered with rooty turf. I enter the darkness.

23

The willow herb's a purple wash
out the corner of my eye. Tall firs rush

up hillsides and are gone. Steadily,
we climb to the river's source as the valley

darkens with heather. The children collapse
into sleep; your head tips back. I fill the gap

between you and the world. The flat-faced owl
clocks me, swivels his head, and hauls

himself up into the stunned air. I wake
at night and wonder whose foot is on the brake.

24

We took him to a house on the coast
(he dreamed) and then were lost

to him for twenty days. He didn't like it
one bit. At night the house slipped

under the sheet of the sea and he slept.
And he dreamed of a clapboard house, tipped

towards the on-coming tide, and of a boy
who sat alone there at a squint window

for whom the sea-light, dying, looked –
and felt – like the closing of a book.

26

You pass through to the world of shades, there to meet
with your former lovers. They stand aside

from their present households, their skin glowing,
their bodies those of the youths you knew.

You cannot speak of the longings that brought you here.
You cannot speak of who your presence might betray.

Your former lovers – palms up – feel for rain;
then return to their homes, to their children.

Mothers with grey flecked hair, who've forgotten
whatever it was you once loved in them.

27

I pack her bags with the most precious things –
love, desire; fear woven through it all like song.

But I don't trust her. I hold up a mirror
to her face. I tell her she's a picture.

But I don't believe in her. She leaves me.
I like to think it's mutual. Now we're both free.

But I find myself thinking of her at night.
My words hover at the edge of prayer.

She knocks on my window, wide-eyed, unslept –
a sprig of vomit in her tangled up hair.

28

I've walked through slaughterhouses,
where birds sing, butterflies jerk through the air.

I've stood beneath shining birch trees,
where bodies tumbled, blood poured over matted hair.

When I move through innocent fields,
horror follows – torture and hidden graves.

I live on blood's doorstep and study
all the ghastliness from which I've been saved.

For this, all the lives I've yet to grieve for
haunt me, as I pass, bearing peace or war.

30

The clouds are high and hard and you are high
above them, looking for that patch of blue

to pass through, through which you'll catch the patchwork
of fields; then a river freckled

with fallen leaves. The ache of fear's so like
the ache of loneliness you had for years –

such a cack-handed gift to yourself! Gripped
by clouds that could rip

your frail craft apart, you sense, as you pass,
a heart flowing free of bitterness at last.

The Football

One spring, Dad came home from school
with an old football the gymies
wanted shot of. A real football, mind –

not one of your plastic ones,
but with a teat that sprang up
from the pink bladder, and trembled

between hexagons of rough leather.
Aye, it's a good one that: which is what
he liked to say of anything

that could bear it. Oh and this ball
had seen service! Did they not
kick ones just like it at the Somme?

I stubbed my toes, launching it
into flower beds where it flattened
all it touched. Then when

lammed into the apple trees,
it rained blossom. Banished at last,
I took it to the park with friends

aware of my limitations.
But then other boys came, laughing
up the slope – confident, at ease.

Any game? His ball. *Can we play?*
I sulked on the line as they kicked
the leather off my ball. Later

I carried it home, a stranger's
bloody head, and threw it, clattering,
deep into the shadows of the hut.

The Card Players

After the luxury of advocaat, lapped
from one-shot glasses held like nuggets
in our fists, we cluster round the orange light
of the paraffin lamp as the cards are dealt.

For a few nights after my aunt and uncle
have left, we'll play on: Sweaty Betty mostly.
Mum loves to say the name. It's terrible!
Like those other words that have escaped

from *Down Below* where language is fiery
or viscous. We are not, I don't think,
a Games Family but play the hands out
as our heavy reading chairs hunker

in the darkness and the lamp's flame
creeps up till a black feather of smoke
presses itself against the glass funnel.
Between hands I make the shortest walk

to the blind gable end of the cottage.
From here ferns thicken to a real darkness
though the track is still held by light swells
of broom. I piss on the grass; my soft

ssh blurring with the steady burr
of the burn. The stars thicken also –
teased-out wool caught on the barbs
of their constellations. For a moment

I'm giddy. When I walk back round
I glimpse the card players past the thin
print curtains; their backs are almost black,
their open faces cut like diamonds

in the lamplight. My cards lie face down
on the table, waiting for me to play them.
Beside them, my father stands, tightening
the top of a hot-water bottle.

Woman Hanging Out the Washing

by Camille Pissarro

Bonnard's wife never aged in his eyes.
Again and again he paints her down the years,
as a filament that lights up her tub,
or svelte as a teenager as she towels
the tall vase of a calf. In recompense

she treated him like shit, his tribute
rather a trap. On the other hand,
Pissarro here takes a break from painting
orchards with flowering fruit trees, peasants
glowing with an earthy vigour, to catch

Madame Pissarro (it's only a guess)
with a child and barrow load of washing.
She is teasing out a sheet on the line
while turning her head to look past her arm
down at the golden-haired toddler, patient

as a book-end, on the warm summer grass.
How *our* mother hated, or said she did,
our father's domestic scenes. To be caught
peeling apples, ironing – uncomposed,
exposed, she felt, in the darg of her day.

What could be less true? 'I am melancholy,
harsh and savage in my works,' Pissarro
exclaims to Lucien, his eldest child
of six; and he pins this woman's profile –
art within art – on the canvas of the sheet.

There's a photograph I took from the kitchen
of our small walled garden on a summer's day;
like Pissarro's, the hedge a full rich green,
nasturtium leaves like lilies and the whole
suffused with a dancing, shadowy light.

It was months before ruined arteries
cost Mum both her legs. Our son crawls across
the patchy grass as *Grandmère* lifts a white sheet
from a blue plastic basket, hands it over
so that you may peg it on the line.

How slow her legs were then! – her feet inching
over the dry earth, yet what reflected joy
was in her insistence to be useful.
Next year she will try gently to explain
to my father they have no Home but this

one room in an old brick house at the end
of a sycamore lane. Young Titi,
if Titi it is, basking in the gaze
of his mother, will die, aged twenty-three
in London, of TB: *our poor Titi*

that we loved so much . . . He was an artist.
And you, Camille, living from hand to mouth,
dressing wounds in sunlight, did your long life
ever look so solid, or a child so safe?
How you must have thought of this moment

and wished you could simply lay down your brush,
scratch your enormous beard and step outside,
not into a world lost to time or to art,
but into the clear light of Pontoise to hoist
that child, one more time, high over your head.

Island Room

In a rambling house on a distant island,
I've heard there's a room, one half of it curtained
from the other by chicken wire. In this half
there's an upturned lobster boat called *Lucky*. Pigeons

use it as a perch; chickens like to roost there. Light
from the windows catches feathers when flight stirs them
or filters through the rusting wire to shine
on the droppings mottling the shell of a boat

the way of lichen on a fallen menhir.
The threadbare chairs are evenly divided, so
you can sit in silence, should you choose, and watch
the world you are coming to and will always reach

in time. Of course it's possible to ignore all this
domestic eccentricity, to put your hand
clean through the wire, to grasp another's, your father's
say, invariably chilled, his nails rough as bark

but the hand itself still the hand of your father,
broad and bearing the ghost of capability,
though you find it lying on his lap like a bird's
limited foot. And you can sit and look where he looks,

and where your mother looks too, at the unfocused
horizon and try to remember all the names
of the wildflowers she taught you: *This is the Star
of Bethlehem, this Thrift, and this Solomon's Seal.*

Now are you listening? And are you listening yet? –
as vase upon vase tips over your outstretched hands,
slips through your fingers – the faded heads and yellowed stems.
From such as these you'll pleat for yourself a mother.

Mostly though you sit in silence as feathers fall
through sunlight till the walls of the room and the room
itself seem the most fragile of ideas. 'Quick now,'
you may have heard your father say at such a time,

'another before your mother comes.' And then both
you and he sink into your chairs, to feel the warmth
of each other's presence – your breathing, his sipping –
your idle thoughts drifting through the grid of days

till his smile latches onto something so fleeting
it's like a feather's caught over his mouth and been
brushed from it in an instant. I think if you were
simply to take a deep breath and walk through the wire

you'd find yourself – as I do – in such a brittle world,
twigs snapping under your feet, gathering themselves
into scattered piles of dusty breaks and fractures,
the stour would catch at the back of your throat or brush

your cheeks like the first warm flurries of snow that come
from nowhere. But soon enough you'd settle to silence,
to those wings folded to perfection, to pink lids closing
on a room I can find no words to leave quietly.

My Father's Funeral

It's the first frosty day in November,
a day pure as a walk along Dornoch beach,
when all the brush strokes are clear – each wave
of sand, of sea, each twirl of wispy cloud –
and your nose to the canvas all the way
to Embo. 'Bonnie.' Aye, bonnie right enough.
Today though, it's the Pennines I cross
to reach you: they lapping, silver on green,
below a sky *you'd* call 'cerulean blue' –

it's almost a shock, Dad, the day's
painted with such a full palette.
Then, arriving at the first staging post
to the grave, in the close family hubbub,
it's no surprise to find you not there,
preferring instead a private moment's
vanity in the long hall mirror, rubbing
your moustache with delight at how black
suits you – you and those flashing brown eyes!

Later, as we wait beside the sleek hearse
'for *Agnes*', you go walkabout again –
an absence you can conjure anywhere
(the tuneless whistle, the stamping dance) –
caught between contemplation of your shoes
and the waiting of a man at the end
of a million accumulated waitings,
a man who can't possibly wait longer –
till, 'Ah, here she comes now. *Michty me!* –

what kept her?' addressing a top-hatted
pall-bearer, his northern accent so rich,
the gravity of the occasion flies from us
and we share a conspiratorial wink.
It's after, I catch you glancing across

at the grave-diggers, leaning on their shovels
under bare oak trees, sharing a joke,
their job half done. And that's where I think
you'd like to be now, anticipating

the punchline, or simply watching them
handle a spade. Country boy at heart,
how you loved to watch anybody
do something well. But, suddenly it's over:
the singing, the prayers, and the tears.
                                You're last
to leave the graveside, turning away,
just when the copper sun angles itself
to perfection; picks out your brass nameplate
and our first scatterings of dry earth.

Poppies

This is how I want to paint,
my mother said and pointed
to her poppies: i.e. not

with any kind of Victorian exactitude –
a timidity that never
dared to interpret

what stood in the vase before her.
Her poppies loom blowsily
out of the frame; strain

on their stems, their pistils golden
with fertility or lust.
                There's nothing
Plathian about them either:

these are no rags, no wounds
shaming the air. They leave
the dead world behind them.

Note how space parts for them
with joy. They are joy. Too heavy
to sway, they nod gently –

Where? Not on Flanders Field
but in a southern breeze –
exotic, bold; precious

as the armfuls of wild white lilies
I bore once round Cape Town
like a swaddled child.

And, as if no heavier
than those lilies, I gathered up
my dead mother,

her face already waxen,
in my arms. Her soul –
lighter still –

rose steadily in the currents
of an unseasonal winter warmth,
fierce as a flame;

free as one of the painted poppies
it had wanted to be
all along.

For the Poets

1. The Bird Man

for Alastair Reid

He is a man fluent
in the language of origami –
an eloquent *esperanto*
of the hands. Present him
with any size or shape
of paper – however flimsy,
however ragged – he'll trim it,
fold it, fashion for you
a bird; in any language,
it's a bird. Personally,
I've observed him
at work in the dark
of a rolling taxi, in the damp-
handed tropics and at a cramped
dinner table with heads nodding
over his articulate hands.
Grip the chest, he'll tell you,
once it's finished, *and gently*
tug the tail. In and out.
In and out. The wings flap;
jerkily, it's true, but still
the bird, in any language,
comes alive. More so
when he says, *All it needs now*
is an eye. Here. And here.
A black dot stares
across the crowded table
from that moment on.
Though all in all,
the making's the thing:
for this bird – this elementary,
unambiguous bird –

lives in *his* hands, chafes
at his fingertips, to be made
flesh, to change meaning,
as it must when it takes
flight for love, or simply
to fill all the moments
when there's nothing better
to do than magic. And this bird,
which has sung for its supper
in so many languages,
in so many circumstances,
is perhaps the smallest
of his many accomplishments,
yet it is, nevertheless, a constant
that flies between languages
with all its possible messages –
and that goes easily and eloquently
where words lie pinioned.

2. Elegy for the Frog Poet

i.m. Norman MacCaig

When you said that was it –
your last word on frogs
and positively too –

that was it for us all. So
when I met a frog one night,
idling at the lights, metallic,

sharp-edged on a wet pavement,
my thoughts turned only
to salvation. Besides

I'd little idea just what
a slippery subject a frog
could turn out to be.

Perhaps it would've sat there,
four-square, for the Frog Poet,
but when I bent to finger

the Braille of its back with second-
hand affections, it shot off
into the squatting queue of cars.

Held now by their lights,
and Buster Keaton white,
I bobbed between them

after my revved-up quarry
like someone caught on a TV
shoot-out. At the very last

I risked offence and grasped
the sand-filled sock of a frog –
no sooner into the action

than spiralling out of it,
as the traffic began to flow;
the frog no sooner mine

than it was leaping the wall
onto the front lawn of a Home
for the Elderly, leaving me,

a split second, frozen
in drizzle, offering an invisible
bouquet to the silent stars.

3. The Haw Bush

i.m. Iain Crichton Smith

At a loch's edge, after heavy rain,
I stood before a haw bush, loosely woven
to let in all the light there was
of a landscape of dark water, dark hills
and darkening autumn sky. Each of its embers

held to the weight of water that hung from it
harbouring the light: each drop
so perfectly poised against the darkness,
the clustered fruits formed a whole
that more than slaked a walker's thirst.

4. The Birthday Party

i.m. Hamish Henderson

After the readings, in the empty hall,
their tweed elbows flowered, their hair took new life.
One sniffed the malty air, fixed, down his fine nose,
the fiddler's eyes with his. 'Play for me, boy.
Play for me.' It was the century's close

and anyone could see they were on the edge
of the Big Time – my jocose sad captains.
With a hedge school to buttress his ancient knees,
one still croaked towards the darkness, with vowels
fervent but drowning, *Freedom Come All Ye!*

from Legacies

'The dead are very demanding.'
Adam Phillips

Every night, for my litany of the dead,
I pluck, with a sleight of hand, the sadness
that hides in kitchen talk. Next day, I'll bless
the dead friends of friends I've never seen –
what can be named won't then overwhelm me.

But Lord, there's no end to the dead!
They make a palimpsest of my list;
each name's closer than the last. They send me
running on errands for items they miss –
to the corner shop for fresh obits and bread.

*

The women of Terezin, brutalised
and fed on slops, transcribed recipes
for Breast of Goose, Plum Strudel, Chocolate Torte
in a *Kochbuch*. Any scraps of paper
they could find were filled with tiny writing

and carefully bound in. Perhaps memory
too marches on its stomach. The simple steps
to a bowl of leek and potato soup –
green coins tumbling from my mother's hands –
is an act of grace to mark my good fortune.

*

In the smoked chill of an autumn morning,
early, my father stands on the back steps,
sharpening my pencils. He holds the black horn-
handled knife lightly and the shaved wood drops
with a glitter of graphite round his shoes.

(His measured strokes made writing my pleasure.)
The penknife snaps shut. My father blows

on each point. His pride. In old age, he'll tut
over faulty wiring and the same knife
will buckle and close to cost him his life.

*

'Come now,' my grandpa said, 'none of your nonsense.
Out with it!' My school reading of *A Man's
A Man* my mother thought was so intense.
Grandpa sipped tea from a saucer as he listened.
I sensed my mother's discomfort for us both.

Near death he sent home his gold watch for me.
On one side of a baroque gold fob, a frisky cock
mounts a hen etched onto an oval stone block
the colour of semen. It took years to pluck them free –
those white heads squawking in the undergrowth.

*

My father's antique rod, unsleeved and cast
over the rivers of the Lothians,
whispered in my ear as I slept. We Pows were
fishermen, it said. Cockenzie, Port Seton,
the herring that coursed through our blood's been lost.

At Cramond, as a boy with hook and line,
I landed an eel. Like a tongue, it writhed,
dying in the dirt, as my line around it
tightened; and all but it ran towards the future
blindly, stitching the river with silver.

*

On Saturday jobs, putting lightbulbs in
for the toffs, *his* dad showed him how power
shaped the Eildon hills, named the dripping woods.
In the thin mist of the Yarrow, the Ettrick
and the Tweed, history was midwife.

Now, scouring a map for ancient names,
testing a circuit to animate the dead,

he hears his own name warm on his father's tongue,
and sees crows rise from an old gable end
as the van's cold engine sputters to life.

*

'August heat. Lost up flaming avenues
of fuchsia – an old railway cottage
where nothing worked. In the fridge the butter
puddled, the tap juddered out dust. At night
I lay, sheetless, too tired to turn the pages

of my book. I thought instead of jars
layered with dried-out caterpillars; of the way
the crabs glowed when we pinned them to the grass,
baking their sweet pink flesh on the sun's spit.
Mother cried for the fortnight. I loved it.'

*

I too remember holidays like that:
the adult talk of what didn't concern us –
damp, dirt, discomfort. And recall how the sun,
catching my jar on the jiggling train home,
fingered me for a killer. But not that one.

That's your memory, though I live there too,
poking crabs on the scorched grass; their salty deaths
somehow shared. Have words ever caught what's true
of you? Nor me. So we'd better advance
by stealth and scuttle crabwise through these lines.

*

Rain trails across a river's curve . . .
In a cupboard, a dead tortoiseshell . . .
On the shelf, Han Shan . . . I wake in a cold room
laid out with a lover's clothes. Each piece calls
out to me with a memory I must tend.

Years before we meet I keep in place
such emptiness that, though I hold the strands
of the tenses and think on you hard,
still I can wake ghostlike in a cold room, rain
on a river . . . the cries of geese, passing . . .

*

There we are on the wet barnacled rock
in thick, belted gabardines, jeans rolled up
at the ankles three times. And we're laughing,
cheeks pouched like apples, with that *adult-
irritant* laughter we just don't want to stop.

Last night I picked three heads of honeysuckle.
Each petal rolled its lip from the pistol
three times over and more; each pink finger's
sole aim to turn itself inside out. So once
we spent laughter like pollen on a dull sea air.

*

Once, shaking him awake, my hand on the rope
of his leg, his grey head slowly surfaced
and he exhaled my name with a sweetness
only those who are truly loved can hope
to hear. Then the smile was gone from his face.

My mother told me he'd call out my name
in distress. Again I knew I was blessed
with love; until the time he set me free –
a stranger. I walked out that sunny room then
and his fierce but fleeting joy passed on to my son.

*

As once you held my life, knowing it all,
so now I hold yours: the gawky girlhood,
bronchitis, wartime cycling with Irene;
the Jenners' meeting with our silent dad,
with his broad artist's hands, his dark-eyed gleam.

And last, the papery breaths, the tilted
head. The day I was born was a beautiful
May day. The hospital window was filled
with blossoms. You kept that memory fresh
for me. Now I fold another into it.

*

All day heat has gathered in the eaves.
I open the attic window to let in
summer's first pressings; and find what breathes
between fresh vats of cut grass and warmed earth's
my Valentine lavender from your bath.

My mother's favourite. Chance keeps a dusty
posy hanging in our kitchen. Rubbed gently,
it still smells faintly of the amnion
you float in, that will live briefly on your lips
as it did on my mother's bunched fingertips.

*

The first summer weeks without the shadow
of their dying. Postcards lie in a packet
on the polished table: one heartbeat
and urgency passes them by. At the foot
of the garden our children play: the Cock Crow,

the Panther padding through his sunlit lair.
Later, as the huge cones of yew darken,
I slip a rotten blue nail from my toe
like a shuffled coin; marvel at the wafer
of light that the air already hardens.

Leaving the House

Whenever we left the house
for any time, Mum liked to leave
a little washing on the line –

a tea-towel, say, or a dish-clout,
just to make people think we were
merely out. Curtains she left

half closed, with blinds half down:
let the unsuspecting who called
around find us half open, half shut –

screening the brightest streaks of light
or keeping a grey day at bay.
But of course anyone who peeked

would know no one could possibly
be living there – each surface
so carefully scoured, the smallest

cloth folded by the sink. Leave it
as you'd wish to return to it
was Mum's motto. But Dad scolded

her in her absence as he packed
and re-packed the car. 'How your mother
thinks all this'll fit . . .' Dad lacked

the patient arts. And it's an in-
complete art, the art of leaving
a house. I hear my own wife start –

'What's keeping you?' while I roam round
our house, twitching at the curtains,
leaving something always undone.

from *Sparks!*
(2005)

Dear Alice

Dear Alice, Thank you for your last letter
with all its glittering tales of wonder.
You made *my* Neverland sound almost dull.
True, I'm in a rut with Hook. We spool
out all that old patriarchal nonsense,
an endless workshop to locate a lens –
a looking glass! – to show us what we are,
why we fight on and on, yet show no scars.
And you? You'll need lifetimes to unravel
the myriad meanings of your marvels.
Wasn't it Freud who said dreams of falling
concerned the act of love? The image rings
such bells with Tinkerbell. (Hope you don't mind –
she seizes all my letters. Zealous, but kind
in her own way, she's at least a regular.)
She took her red pen and fairy ruler
across all that nibbling and tasting too –
she claims both you and the White Rabbit knew
what he'd lead you to. Me, I'm captain
of my own ship, absolved from time's stain,
though I'll never step ashore. The sun
sinks now over these soft green hills.
Muffled, I hear geese's meaningless calls.
Somewhere, I've missed out on love, dear Alice.
Wendy tells me I don't know how to kiss.

To Kafka on My Wedding Anniversary

Charles Bridge, Prague: 9 April 2002

Once more I think of you, walking alone
across this bridge after an evening's
laying bare, your life metamorphosing
into the conundrums you'll leave us with:
        while on the bridge

the statues darken, casting off their vows
of sanctity and hope, till they too become
deathly shadows. Yet for the young soldier,
this spring afternoon, pinned by his lover
        against the bridge –

his beret, two palm leaves held in one hand,
the black plinths of his boots, her harbour –
the choices seem natural as white swans
turning in the river between the spans
        of a sunlit bridge.

Beside these youths, St John of Nepomuk,
green with age, rises over the reliefs
on which he acts out his fate. The pilgrims'
touch has turned them to gold. Where the martyr's
        cast from the bridge

I too touch – for the luck of love – his chest.
It was a different kind of luck, which gave
to St Lutgard her cinematic visions
of Christ's five gaping wounds to kiss. And a
        different bridge

that led the self-flagellants to follow
St Vincent – it seems each must be wedded
to something. And it's a different order
of luck entirely, for us all, that in the
        absence of bridges

you could cross, you took your work (your life)
as your only wife. Jasmine, magnolia
and cherry blossoms roll over this town.
Yesterday, in sunshine, a wedding couple
          crossed the bridge –

it looked the easiest of difficult things.
The cameras turned from the stone faces
and joined the procession, as a light snow fell
from blue skies: each flake a hands-breadth apart
          kissed the bridge goodbye.

Sleepless

In *medianoche*, they find themselves –
a father and his two children,
unable to sleep through the ever-
gathering heat of themselves –
sitting in their pants
round the kitchen table, a plastic flagon
of fridge-cold water emptying
before their eyes. There is something
secretive meeting like this –
the children's naked chests
brushing the table's edge, as upstairs
their mother sleeps on,
wound in her tangle of sheets.
Though, whatever the secret is,
it remains unspoken, shared
like a scent of hilltop thyme.
If, that is, a scent could be seen
through a film of sleep –
in the way, just say, the boy had earlier
watched his sister from below the surface
of the pool, as she wind-milled
into water, hair flaring
above her, the water giving her
the graceful movements
of the dancer she is. Moments later,
he had popped up, raising goggles, wiping eyes.
How did I look? she'd asked. *How did I look?*

They sit composed now, slightly slumped,
sculpted by the kitchen light, as the moon
gives shape to the olive trees, the stones
in the fields, the fallen almonds. They are a family,
once all activity has been stripped from them.
And they sit, mostly in silence, sifting through
this air, this love, the faintest scent of thyme.

Blessings, Havana

My grandfather was a sailor
as solid as his name – Sam Black. Bless him.

This Sunday morning, before the sun's
even settled in the sky, he sports

a Masonic frown for his grandson,
chugging across the gift of the bay

which made this city in a rusted
old pontoon. I'm on a pilgrimage

to the neat and airy kirk
of Nuestra Señora de Regla –

there to pay homage, in my own way,
to the Virgin of Regla, patron saint

of sailors and of Yemayá,
Santeria goddess of the sea,

both one and the same. Bless
those who can share their gods –

they give hope to us all; proof surely
no god will be known wholly

by one sect, convocation, Concordia
or General Assembly. As the priest

relaxes to his sermon, like a man
constantly searching for a question,

a stream of supplicants cross
the transept to the small chapel

where the black-faced virgin
holds her crowned and dainty white doll.

They light candles
for the crucified Christ at her side

but for Yemayá,
whose attributes are the sun and the moon,

they bring flop-headed sunflowers,
buckets of gladioli and roses.

Bless prayer, poetry and praise; the lighting
of candles, the bringing of flowers –

bless whatever it takes, be it
the warming glow of a computer screen,

that gives us pause to think.
She wears a white ruff like spume

around her face, a silver crown,
a cloak of Caribbean blue.

Bless the skiff that sails on it –
each barque, clipper and tanker;

each no more than a spark
on its endless pleats. Bless language

which brought me here and the silence
beyond blessing which is beyond

language's reach. Bless twice the twin scar
that furrows my wife's belly

out of which our children came.
My grandfather was a sailor, Sam Black by name.

Bless him. Bless her. Bless them. And bless
this sacred earth – in couplets without end.

Amen.

from *Transfusion*
(2007)

from Transfusion

II

'Five bucks if you can lay a hand on me,'
Ali had said and the way Mark tells it
you can tell he knows this is a golden moment
for his father and in the lives

of all the men there: Ali, passing through
a hot little town in the South, sometime
in the three year lay-off, exiled but never far
from people's thoughts. 'What does it profit me

to be the wellest-liked man in America
who sold out to ev'body?' Big blue-grey Cadillac
just stopped there fore a clapboard store front –
and there he was! Ali, shuffling in the dust,

spoofing. Oh the men threw their punches all right,
but slight ones, for who'd want to hurt him
in daylight like that? The tallest, prettiest
man around. His retinue leaning back

into the cool shadows, smiling too, everyone
at ease, feeling his ease, easy like he was
some kinda king who'd revealed himself
to his people. 'You'll never guess what?'

the men said in the bars that night and again
to their wives as they slipped their overalls off.
'Yeah, this hand here. Took it and shook it.'
And in memory there was always something

about the quality of the light that day,
like even in the hot South, it was brighter,
clearer, in tune with the blue of their overalls
and the blue in his skin as that fist

had whipped at them. 'Came outa nowhere – pop!
Fast? Man, you kiddin? Ain't never seen nothin
like it ma born days.' Pop! Pop! Pop! But oh,
it had brushed their cheeks like a caress.

IV

'They out there cheerin cause their blood
is pourin into somebody they love.
Transfusion. It's got to make you cry.'
            Drew 'Bundini' Brown

It's got to make you cry –

how in training, a child turns from him
and buries his face in his mother's neck,
terrified by the mean-man mouth, puckered
round the gum shield, the sweating face framed
by the black helmet, gloved fists the size
of cannonballs; till he removes
the gum shield, lifts off the helmet, and smiles
that conniving Ali-boy smile, that sets
the boy himself laughing, letting himself
be lifted high in those huge bandaged hands,
Ali whispering things in his ear
only the boy and his mother can hear.

And we see all that crushed –

for how can the fine things survive Foreman's
sledgehammer fists? *His* is the way of the world –
we know it in the night – sure to triumph
over Artistry, Gentleness and Love.
We see a dancer, we see Poetry,
Elegance – the darting lead and he's gone.
We see Cleveland 'The Cat' Williams pawing
clear air, as Ali shuffles the dimensions
before him, in the days he fought with his legs –
so fast, man, could 'turn out the light . . .

be in bed fore it's dark.' Such nights,
it wasn't boxing, more vaudeville – *with blood.*

And that's getting to the heart of the matter –

for what we so admire is technique, a sense
of form; not the thing itself – the fist crashing
into Terrell's face again and again:
the cobra jab that came in triplets –
'Say ma name! Say ma name! *Say it!'*
and the misery might then be over.
Over fifteen rounds making a puzzle
of Ernie's eyes; commentators wishing
in the end the Champion more gracious,
more *compassionate.* 'Don't care how bad
ma hands hurt,' he says of this fight. 'I'll hit him
till the pain tears them off at the wrists.'

Oh yes, brother, be not deceived,
the badness *too is part of the brew.*

X

That's when Frida Kahlo, twenty years dead,
but with a lifetime too full of pain and joy ever
to be free, or to hold her peace with the dead,
felt their power and decided to come back

down one of the conduits of blood
that was still open to her, fresh as a wound,
to paint them both – Ali and Mandela –
a double portrait in their prime.

It's a portrait neither of boxer nor
of politician but of two equal spirits
who have met on crossing roads. Their hands
touch, but lightly; there's no call

to make more of the moment. Rather
there's an ease between them both. Mandela's
face is the one the world knew: square, dark,
that straight parting, the eyes narrowing

in a smile. Ali's face has the beauty it has
in repose. *So pretty.* Kahlo's surrounded them
with the strongest familiars – tiger, cheetah,
monkey and gazelle. Bluebirds dart

between them and, of course, butterflies
and bees. Bright green, black and yellow flowers
adorn them; mark them out as fighters, brothers.
Through their warm eyes, Frida Kahlo outfaces death.

from *Dear Alice: Narratives of Madness*
(2008)

Prelude

It's one of those mornings
when it's a blessing to be
up and about. The chestnuts
wear the early light with grace,
the grass is silver with dew.

A young, tawny cat pads
over the path before him –
in its mouth, the early
morning sparrow, its beak still
soundlessly praising the day.

Inauguration

He casts an eye round the brightly painted room –
the perfect pot plants, the prints on the walls,
the audience at their tables
down to their last sips of wine.

'Let us remember,' he begins, 'what's most remarkable
about the very room we're in tonight –
only last year it was home
to the criminally insane.

And we're delighted,' he continues,
'that some of them
are able to join us now.'

They shuffle in – the criminally insane.
One carries a sparrow jammed in his mouth;
one swishes a dead chicken through a spill
of blood-red wine. The crowd

eases back, not wishing
to cause offence, demonstrating more
than a clear willingness to share the space
with its former inmates.

We are a *Liberal* Arts College, after all.

But the criminally insane have a spokesperson too,
a small man with electrified hair,
who wishes us to know what's most
remarkable about this space

is how many of the dead
once moved here. 'So please, with me,
welcome back the dead.' And the dead
mooch in, lifting their heavy lids to the light.

They look around, approvingly it's clear,
at the decor, at us and at the fidgeting
criminally insane. 'Remarkable . . .

'Remarkable . . .' the chairman repeats
as a sound of thunder fills the air
and the foundations
start to shake.

Nebuchadnezzar in the Arboretum by Moonlight

Nothing but madness till now, the hard earth
callusing my hands, the snow and the rain
seeping through cracked skin. Though it was birth
of a kind at first to leave far behind
that other madness – my name on each brick
of the city, each flower willed into place
by me – and to fall on all fours, to lick
dirt, let it mat with the hair of my face.

But let those who can still read, read the signs:
cherry trees stand amazed in their own moons
of blossom, while I root through the rich wines
of the earth. I'll excavate a new song
to last till my empire falls. Let all fall –
apart from these trees and one well-lit hall.

From Foucault: Two Tales and a Bedlam Ballad

1. Appetite

A man, believing himself to be dead,
stopped eating. The world became a plaything

of shadows. Spectres haunted him daily.
But Death, he discovered, was thin gruel –

there was no nourishment to be found there.
In for the long haul, he took to his bed.

Dying, however, remained active long after
he'd thought it disarmed. Nothing for it

but to soldier on till the cupboard
of memory was bare. A few of his friends

disguised themselves. They whitened
their faces then shrouded their forms

in loose-fitting black gowns. They entered
his room, set up a table before him

and brought to it a spread of bread, meat,
cheese, chocolate and wine. They ate and drank

then replenished the feast. He stared at them
from out of the hollows of his fading eyes.

But why, they asked him, did he stay in bed?
Didn't he realise dead people eat as much

as the living ever did? They helped him
up and they ate together through the night.

As dawn broke, they rejoiced at his rebirth –
the colour that flooded his cheeks; the energy

with which he cracked a chicken wing apart.
Yet they wondered, as they rose from the table,

how he'd lit the hunger in their bellies
that drew them back to these splintered bones.

2. The Wise Farmer

It was said, between Tinwald
and Torthorwald, lived a farmer
who could cure the mad. A Hercules
of a man, he yoked two to the plough –

and if one shrugged at the traces
he larded the stick across his back.
They were kept naked
and dark as the earth itself

and, as the plough thrust in –
cleaving to one side clods,
roots and rocks – the tendons
of their necks were guyed like ropes,

the clenched muscles of their flanks
clear as if they'd been flayed.
In the cloudbursts of spring,
blindly they lifted their faces

and the rain washed them
like stones. They were as nothing
from where the rains came – as peewits
in the vast open rigs of sky.

Madness, the farmer instructed
his neighbours, is the bestial
raised in man. The trick's to restore
to man the animal that rages

in his heart. With Reason beaten,
docility's assured. Below Torthorwald,
come evening, the Lochar Moss
is groomed with gold. He unshackles

his pair and leads them to the byre.
After feeding, they crouch down
together in their stall. They tend
the raw burns on their shoulders,

the welts across their backs. Neighbours
claim they hear them howl – insist their door
is firmly snecked. Still the wise farmer
has his champions and it's said,

if you travel between Tinwald
and Torthorwald, it's hard to tell
which half of the men might be beasts –
or which of the beasts be men.

3. Glass

Because I'm made of glass,
I must beware I break.
Because I'm made of fire,
I can't give back what I take.

Because I'm made of water,
I must cup every drop.
Because I'm made of iron,
I must cradle other crops.

Because I'm made of ice,
I must keep out the sun.
Because I'm made of pain,
I keep away from guns.

Because I'm made of love,
I find I'm haunted nightly.
Because I'm made of grass,
I must move surely, lightly.

Because I'm made of feathers,
I must not fear to fall.

Because I'm made of fear,
you must come when I call.

Because I'm made of memory,
I live in an endless forest.
Because of appetite and will,
I must be always polished.

Because I'm made of earth and ash,
I keep my head bowed down.
Because I'm made of hope,
I sew my wedding gown.

Because I'm made of piss and shit,
I must live by grace alone.
Because I'm made of wheat and chaff,
I bide between two stones.

Because I'm made of air,
I've had to learn to share.
Because I'm made of darkness,
I rely on others' prayers.

Because I'm made of off-cuts,
I must write my own story.
Because I'm made of light,
I will not ration my glory.

Night Watch, 1842

When night falls and all others
have resigned their trust, I walk
the galleries, the guardian,
the master of all that stalks
their fitful sleep. I inquire
into all complaints, gratify
all reasonable desires.
I compel those with angry

and turbulent passions
to follow healthier trains
of thought. I give due ballast
to the most frivolous claims –
become master of reason
when I've need to flatter
the restless and the noisy:
'What spikes your night are *pictures*,'
I tell them. One's convinced
that shadows cut her like knives,
another dreams she's beset
by gangs of wizards and thieves.
To those who sing or whistle
or laugh; or to one who struts
the long gallery and chants,
'Dirty slut, dirty slut, slut . . .'
I'll bring the required balm.
The somnambulist I'll lead
back to bed like a child;
while to her who cries for 'Auld
Auntie Peggy', my soft step
nears like a loved one,
giving fresh hope and healing
to her troubled mind. No sound
soils the night that can't be traced
back to its primary source.
From their soliloquies, songs
and prayers, I chart the course
of that wayward black river
whose stream's one moment choked
by rock and, at the next, split
in shallows featureless as smoke.
In the solitude of midnight
I notate such fractured plots.
When day commands the gallery,
another will take my watch.

The Last Vision of Angus McKay

Angus McKay, Queen Victoria's piper, went insane 'over study of music'. He was admitted to the Crichton Royal from Bedlam in 1856 when he was 43 years old.

'His most prominent delusion is that Her Majesty is his wife and that Prince Albert has defrauded him of his rights.'

Crichton case notes

Let it be noted (in copperplate), Angus McKay
is a gentleman to watch. The stoutest furniture
is firewood to him; a mattress, within a day,
he'll disembowel. He has been known
to drink his own urine; to spit, shriek, howl
and hoot like an owl:

> though this last
> does not appear
> in his case notes from Bedlam –
> 'hooting and howling' in southern parts
> being thought not
> abnormal for a Scot.

Nevertheless, there is enough on his native ground
to amaze and perplex his keepers.

Fuck it! Angus McKay has done with them all.

He eases himself into the rivercold waters of the Nith
across which lies Kirkconnell Wood
and his freedom. At that moment

> (to which the record is blind,
> no body being found, never mind
> testament forthcoming)

something catches his eye – a sudden flurry and a bird
with two necks intertwined; one black, the other –
bodiless – a shimmering Islay malt brown.

Angus McKay watches, mesmerised

as the cormorant lifts its white-cheeked head
till its brassy twin – the eel – lifting with it,
unwinds like a flailing clef and falls, bit by bit,
into perfect darkness.

This, thinks Angus McKay, is how
the bagpipe has devoured my life.

He lies on his back, drifting downstream,
shadowing the black bag of a bird through flanges of light,
past two gracefully disinterested swans. The eel rages still –

the cormorant's neck rising and falling
in a helpless hiccup. Up ahead, the bird will calm,
its neck settle again on its shoulders –

but there, the quicksand waits to welcome Angus McKay,
sipping him, limb by limb, into its dark and clammy hold.

That evening, owls will keen – in Gaelic –
from Kirkconnell Wood, where Angus McKay
perches, pale and dripping.

Will a soul never find peace? he asks.
Oh, where has my plump little lover gone –
and what's become of that shit, Prince Albert?

Field Notes

I found a woman, squatting
by a peat fire in the centre
of a bare room. With the exception

of a piece of old bag worn
like a shawl, she was quite naked
above the waist. The house itself

is near to tumbling in
around her – ruinous, wretched,
comfortless: both wind and rain

have free entrance. Nor can words
do justice to the filth, dirt,
confusion and so on

and so forth. Vermin, faeces,
ruinous smells – you've read it
all before: how she

cannot tell the day
or the hour or count the fingers
on her hands, how she understands

nothing of religious truth. She lives
it is said on a cat's piss
of milk, yet still

monthly calls the children
around her, holding up two
red fingers like a flag.

Her husband has no words
but is capable of a growl
whenever he feels threatened

or excited. His habits –
dirty also: gapes, slavers, squints etc.
Words fail. Will not wash

but would embrace fire.
In good weather, nothing better
than to be led into a paddock

behind the stockyard. Here
he rolls incessantly (it is said)
a large stone (it is said)

from one end of the enclosure
to the other, till his hand (always
the right) (it is said) bleeds.

These unfortunates only meet here
as parents of a girl, blind at birth,
who crouches by a window

endeavouring (it is said)
to seek out the fugitive light
as it enters a broken pane.

The Buoy-Tree

Lochans of rain gathered
in the hollows, the trees
were dripping and bare.

On one, a gull landed,
spreading its wings like an angel.
It must have been a sign –

for angels are signs if nothing else.
Soon other gulls flocked there
till the whole tree was frocked

with them. Their wings beat
the water gently from them,
touching each other as you might

brush your arm against another
in a dance. It's a wonder
you never saw it that day,

it was all there was really to see –
a tree that seemed to writhe
with light, like a buoy

on a featureless sea.
But what drew the birds there,
or set them back in flight,

is just one more thing at which
to wonder. I can only think
it was the rain that kept you away.

Tryst

Watercolour by I (or J) Bannerman (c. 1861)
'In three of the productions, representing spots and transactions
in the Highlands, and imbued with the most brilliant and blazing
colours, the story told is merely stupid and Quixotic.'

Dr Browne in *Mad Artists*

The tree twists
like a brown flame
fresh from the earth,

its stubby branches
end in green whorls
like fists. They

grasp an anger
that rages around them –
the wind-whipped grasses,

the clutch of reeds,
sturdy as swan's necks,
ready to strike.

A young woman's climbed
to this fruitless tree, trailing
her long green gown.

She turns to the tree
her blood-red cheeks,
the impassive wound

that is her mouth: the whites
of her eyes are intent
as arrows or as seeds.

Indeed, how fierce
must this tortured tree be
before she'll look away,

one arm still held
across her long green gown
as above

the impenetrable
cocoons of clouds
scud by.

Questions of Judgement

The Crichton Home Farm Steading, 1891

Everything here has its proper place –
grain in the granary, cows in their stalls,
carts parked in the dark arcades.

There each can be judged – the weight of grain,
the yield of cows, the greased wheels'
turning. And how easily

such judgements are made. Take
the Ayrshire bull, standing now
in the shadowy yard, his back

straight, forehead broad, rump
'level and long from hooks to pin-bones' –
no arguing with any of that.

Or that it's the proper place
of the farm manager, in cloth cap
and waistcoat, to hold the fine head

at show height, as another, almost
his twin, stands proudly – fists on hips –
at his side. Meanwhile

in the fields beyond, the 'pauper
lunatics' labour. They are judged
by simple needs: a plenitude of food,

fresh air and exercise. Each evening
heading home, the huge clock-face
confronts them like a new moon

binding them to the slow seasons
of growth. *God Send Grace.*
At night each, like a beast in the stall

of an almost-endless byre, watches
shadows from the dying fire play
on the ceiling. Some graze then

on a world beyond measure. Others
recoil, wondering in spite of it all, when
and just where they will ever fit in.

Deirdre

Because she was Deirdre,
Deirdre was simply who she was
and the world was dark
as an apple cellar, each apple
rotten to the core. So who
could she turn to, cast
down the steps, all alone
in the darkness, her small hands
feeling their way along damp walls
as she moved between those boxes
and boxes of shrivelled, soft fruit? Still,
their sweetness called to her
and in the middle of each, she found,
past the waste of broken flesh,
five seeds, counting them out
on her fingers. She sang to them
of apples on a summer day,
shining in sunlight. She stroked
the tiny back of each one,
as it sat like a dark little flame
on her fingertip. Then she patted
the seed into a scraping of earth
at her feet. And she prayed
the apple prayer which calls
for a commonwealth of apples
to be shared wherever
there is earth and sunlight.
And the multiples of seeds grew
till shoots became seedlings
and seedlings trees – trees
whose thirsty crowns thrust
through the darkness of the cellar
and opened into light. Borne up with them
and dancing now from crown to crown,
gathering apples in her skirt
was Deirdre –
Deirdre of the Apples.

The Wolf Man at Crichton Hall, 1914

'In my story what was explained by dreams?
Nothing as far as I can see.'

The Wolf Man, quoted in *The Wolf Man Sixty Years After,*
Karin Obholzer, 1982

The window opens in winter
and I am a child once again,
drawn by shouts, as I was back then,

to look out on a Christmas tree,
new-felled on the estate and brought
to my own window-side, for me.

But there are no baubles this time,
no angel glittering on top.
Instead on the silent branches

of a chestnut tree stand seven
white wolves, their eyes the sole candles,
their tails the only tinsel.

Time stops with seven white wolves.
Though a couple adjust their paws
from one branch onto another,

their broad heads stay perfectly still,
staring into the room where I stand
frightened to break this privilege.

For years I saw my mother thus,
four-legged and caught in moonlight.
For a moment without language

our eyes locked. Shame, anger or fear –
I felt the power of seven
times seven white wolves to wish me

away. But I've not been woken
by that image in years. Now,
looking at their wedding picture,

at her body in its white sheath,
pliant and ready for his, I share
nothing but her joy. No matter –

the seven white wolves still return
to stand in cold moonlight, to meet
my questioning gaze. I'm told now

they are images, conjured
from seven calico nightshirts
hung on a line. But I ask you,

if these are calico nightshirts,
then where are the seven white wolves
that were there in their place? They pad

along the frozen paths, between
Rutherford and Carmont, between
Dudgeon and Monreith, in the dark

ellipses of the night. And, while
these white nightshirts bandage the breeze,
seven white wolves howl at the moon.

And no, my mother did not howl.
And no, my father did not howl.
This is not a dream about love,

but about a sister tree, torn
from the old estate. Soon this one
will be brought, bleeding, before me,

hung with ribbons of flesh; while wolves
scavenge between Ypres and the Somme,
between Paschendale and Verdun.

Service Patient, 1916

Even in the cold dark days,
when Criffel's no more
than a black outline – a crouched

and headless beast – he prefers
to sit out on the veranda, to be
without walls. In the November *New Moon*

he reads a report from Miss McLeod,
matron on the *St Andrew* – a hospital ship
on the Rouen to Southampton run.

'There is nobody on earth,' she writes,
'like the British Tommy.
        Never
        a growl
        or a grumble;
        a limb off
        is nothing.
        They are so glad
        so surprised
        to be alive.
        Dear, brave boys . . .
        nothing's
        too good for them.
        A delicate slip
        of a boy of nineteen
        in today's load
        going home
        to his mother
        with his right leg
        and right arm
        off. It's
        heartbreaking
        yet she may

consider
herself
and him
lucky.'

He looks up.
                    Red-flagged ships
push end to end up the River Nith
as far as they can go. No longer can they

hold back the maimed and the wounded
from the farms and the villages which call them.
Up the narrow roads or stumbling

over the furrowed fields, through the hedges
they cannot see, they come at him,
falling, then rising, from the furrows,

the trenches and the fruitless briars.
Their writing hands are bandaged stumps.
They wave them in the frosty air.

Nurses

They took off their uniforms –
after all, it was so hot, the seams so stiff –

and lay them on the grass
like semaphores. The sun

beat on their young breasts,
till their skin cracked and flaked,

the way of wood on the prows
of old boats. (I could take you now

to two or three that have sunk in river mud
and lie there, useless and unloved.)

So they stood, like wood themselves,
facing autumn with fortitude,

till all fruit had fallen from them
and children cut their names –

Megan, Danny and *Frank* –
deep into their bark.

Freud at the Crichton

Home movie, September 1939

The invitation had come from one
of the younger exiles: 'Head north,
if you can, however briefly.

The blandness of a schnitzel
wouldn't be out of place
on any menu here and there's work –

Lord, there's a whole nation
waiting for the couch.' All true
of course, but he'd felt

suddenly tired in the well of the hall
where, even behind wire mesh,
the chatter of the patients (incessant,

driven) had reminded him
of the *Kaffeehaus* – everyone bent
over frothy coffees; all of them lipping:

Kraft-Ebbing, Kraft-Ebbing, Kraft-Ebbing.

So it is in the Crichton grounds
we see him, come to watch
Jumbo, the Pekinese, run the run

that looks like a no-legged dash.
Even in grainy black and white,
which tricks us all into a jaunty grace,

he is composed – his right arm
crooked to his waist, in the left
hand a trademark cigar, his wrist

as slender and knuckled as any
in Egon Schiele. His cancerous mouth
is a pencil-thin shadow of pain.

Braver hund, Jumbo, braver hund.

Inside slicks of sunlight had fallen
from high windows, taken him back
to his rooms in Berggasse, the irony

that, in emptiness, they were finally
filled with light. Himself, he sees
as an interruption to the light

that will fill his space so very soon.
Though swifts tailor the air
with momentary designs that read like joy,

for him, there is no room for any
but very ordinary happinesses – the cigar,
the dog, the arm of Martha, his wife.

Together, they wander the nations –
Chestnut, Sycamore, Lime and Birch.
It's an early autumn here. He shivers

and they both head back up the path.

Grass

1. The Weaver

Is it true there's a man who makes clothes
out of grass? Yes, if it's long enough he makes
clothes out of grass. Where can you find them,
these garments of grass? Look beneath the holly hedge,
below the skirts of rhododendron. He takes little care
to hide them. So who are they for – these boots,
this jacket and vest, woven in grass?
They are for the weaver's own joy and to praise
the industry of hands. (They are also
for whichever of God's creatures
may find a use for them – mice
and small birds come readily to mind.)

2. The Iceman

Of course there were those who told him,
    before he took off for the mountain pass,
that to survive all the snow and the jagged ice
    he'd need more than a coat woven from grass.

But he simply dons his coat of grass
    and his conical grass hat. They see him
like something from a fair. *Man Made of Grass.*
    Then – even more the scarecrow –

he bends to his skin boots and crushes in
    as much as he can of – you guessed – more grass.
A-ha, so he knows about skins? They all do –
    he and those who look on him now, lost

in amazement. They're draped in furs –
    the silver fur of a fox, the dark roast of a bear,
the fleeces of flocks fed on the rich grass
    that grows in the valley, before the forest masses

on the slopes where the hunters find their purpose
    and their songs. Their hearts come alive
with the blood-world around them. Grass
    has no god: this man is tinged with madness.

So when they see him leave the valley floor,
    they wave him off and feel their future blessed
with the power of the beasts they shoulder.
    There goes a sad man, they say, helpless as grass.

He never tells them his heart's caught in a fork
    between high branches; no one'll reach
where it rests in its nest of withered grass.
    He froze to death of course: nobody's loss.

Thousands of years later, an 'Iceman' is found,
    perfectly preserved on a mountain pass.
On a stone ledge beside him, plaited from grass,
    lies a rope, coiled like a noose.

3. Rashin-Coatie

Let's interrupt the story, take time out.
Soon she'll go to the palace to seek work.

Soon she'll meet the prince and sure as day
marry him. She's living with the red calf for now –

the favourite she refused to kill, the one
who bore her away, naked, on his back.

Click-a-clack, click-a-clack, click-a-clack –
legs round your belly, rump on your back.

The calf's long pink tongue's latched
round some rushes by a loch. From them

she's woven a coat of sorts. Each day
the same palace guards laugh in her face

as they turn her away. Each night
she remembers her father dwelling

on her worthlessness, recalls
her sister's head falling in the sack.

Click-a-clack, click-a-clack, click-a-clack –
why would I ever ever want to go back?

Easier to thole, the years with the old bull,
his hot breath, his royally indifferent eye.

This then is her life, an interrupted story –
every day her hands held out,

her coat, long brittle, revealing
the remorseless narrative beneath.

Don Quixote

'Today he's the unhappiest creature
in the world, the poorest too, and
tomorrow he'll have two or three
kingdoms to hand over to his squire.'
Miguel Cervantes, *Don Quixote*

For whatever reason, it's common
that, after years of obstinate madness,
the mind recomposes itself. Women,
whose very names once gave the soul purpose,

become mired in time with the rest of us.
In this brief breathing space before the end,
our lives' adventures seem ridiculous:
the losses they brought too late to amend.

But still it falls to poor Don Quixote
to put right to himself and his companion
the wild falsehoods he mistook for glory.

'Don't die,' Sancho pleads with the failing don.
Now he would exchange, for one last story,
three kingdoms on which the sun never shone.

Resistances

from female admission notes, 1839

1.

each duty commands its own song
this gives it roots in the instant

while I polish while I sew
I give growth to what I do

*

you can hide under the eaves of song

in the same way
the heart of a spring crocus
beats secretly in its green sheath

*

laughter too lends a generous shade
it will be received unquestioned   rootless as the wind

*

I am indifferent to objects   unless
I can act upon them   in stealing
a pair of scissors   in concealing
a silver brooch   I find something
of what I am
                a thin ravaged edge
it is this
which I do not wish to return

*

it is not important that you
find me   I dance

from one end of the room to the other
I circle myself
till exhaustion claims me

*

I recast radiance
like a May tree in bloom

2.

because you dig the garden
it doesn't mean
you don't think the sky will fall in

it's only a position like any other

your foot on the fork
its tines smoothing through the earth

    *

look at the dark horizon
or wait for the horizon to darken

    *

who are my enemies

they have been as an army
will wash over the land

and leave some still digging

the fields red with blood
the turnips good

    *

I have found a little shade
beyond here the world burns

you are best to keep silent
no one likes to hear bad news

    *

where is nowhere to move on to
from here   no   I will not pretend
any more   nor let you

3.

home has lost our touch
and so is lost to us

these annual visits
do nothing

but prove the distance travelled
is too great

                    *

the dressing table   the cooking spoon
the light slanting through the window

we are not where they are   nor do we
see ourselves in them

                    *

the world too has lost our touch
so we are the least deceived
the most free to act   where we

see flames we will say so
where the world drowns we will not avoid it

                    *

our own bodies leave us

                    *

from secret hidey-holes we watch
them hopelessly embracing
their own exile

4.

I watch

while the world punishes itself   it gives up
birds to fall from its sky   blossoms

to be torn from its trees   love
that it may be humiliated

*

the seas rage but they give up
                    their dead all the same
forests eat light to live on in darkness

*

a tide will dash the limbs
from a crab and still the crab lives on

waiting for a gull to find it

*

I lose no more

than the world loses daily   the tide
is drawing from it and I am left

a crab spitting on the foreshore

*

understand this   my only hope
was to become stone

5.

how many steps in any direction
are to be trusted   the answer is three

*

beyond these three

there is an infinite number
of dangers which could befall you

nor beyond three steps
can you trust to your own innocence

*

for both these reasons you take
three steps with a constant mourning

as if you were a tree
with a wind weaving through its branches

     *

it is well to know the world
over which you have command

a core where you can stand and say
what happens here is all I know

     *

stamp out all other dreams

     *

I will let into my world
three things   air   light

and the trapped sparrow
matron took a brush to

6.

you make a bargain with the world
you say   I am not worthy of being on the earth

the world says   *work*

sew polish clean   *read widely but wisely*

     *

you make a confession to your husband
you say   there are times when I wished you dead

he says   *work*

sew polish clean   *read widely but wisely*

     *

in each activity you bless this house
but not yourself in it   the river

waits if only you could escape

*

a stranger saves you   you sit
on the riverbank to gather your breath

small birds dance on the sandbank
and watch the sea tide coming in

*

you want only one thing

that the world would efface you

7.

to remain yourself   deny yourself

*

the world recognises a fire
by its flames   rather

think of yourself as a calm sea
that cannot be mapped   no one

will wish it harm   few will care
what happens under its surface

*

the trick is not to care yourself   to live
truly in the negative spaces

she does not even   she neither seeks nor
she never calls upon

*

the world moves with you
in this denial of light   as night falls

allow yourself the murmur
of a prayer   it is your duty to silence

that ensures you will be heard

*

over the frosted bulbs of the earth

ruins   brevity   dust

8.

lost soul there is a world
to be part of   all it takes is time

*

the accretions you have taken
to be your life did not reach

their ripeness in a day   how can you
hope to shed them in so short a time

*

if you embrace your exile
you will surprise yourself at what

can be so quickly lost   flesh
anger   memory   the storehouses

that flamed your life   you have bartered
their contents for this tranquillity

*

destitute of volition   free as a sea plant
you float with the disinterested tide

*

hold back only a small
mournful cry for the night and determine
that by your shit at least
they will know you

9. Coda

speak for me in a small voice
something indistinct that you might hear

on a forest walk but deep
in the darkness off the track   don't

*

speak with understanding   if you do
you've misunderstood what I am

*

look at the moon through the branches

there is almost music as the clouds
cover it   then let it go

*

that is not the moon I'm looking at

*

neither are you
the one to speak for me   not even daring

to raise your voice in the darkness

*

I could tell you things   oh
the things I could tell you   but again

you would sift them through the grid
of your understanding and then

you would not be speaking for me

*

which is all I ask
this clouded evening   that somewhere

in the silence   there is someone
who speaks   with indifference

in a small voice
for me

The Great Asylums of Scotland

The great asylums of Scotland, cloistered
like the proud abbeys we tore down brick
by brick. Yet harder to love. They docked
at the edge of our towns like relations
with whom we felt ill at ease. Ones who kept
themselves to themselves. Their farms. Their laundries.

Their water supplies. We stand in their portals,
our eyes drawn down the tree-lined avenues
to the prospect of distant hills. Country houses?
Hydros? Oh, what shall we do with them? –
the great asylums of Scotland, still with us,
as keen to serve as the day they were built.

A fleet for their time they set out, freighted
with hope and grand design. Look at them now,
scuttled on the ocean floor. Light floods them.
Along their corridors, doors flap open
on empty cabins with nothing to hide.
In attic rooms the sky's light pours over

a tide-wrack of maps, plans, records – a grid
to lay over a waste of rage, grief, anger
and pain. None of that will make a cairn.
In these, the great asylums of Scotland,
always it is evening about to fall.
The heavy doors are closing on us all

and the counting begins. But coming through
the frayed web of darkness are slants of light:
greenness, firstness, hope. What is to be done
with a two-faced legacy such as this?
Multi-occupancy – that's the answer!
Flatpacks to the gentlemen's quarters,

IKEA to the boardrooms. Four by fours
draw up before the great asylums now.
They're made for them, framed by chestnut trees,
like adverts. Inside the auction hall –
the stillness of graveyards, the discretion
of private affairs. Oh how beautiful

are the crafted dovetails in the wardrobes
no one wants. They sulk like small monuments
history has ignored. So much gloom.
'I wouldn't want any of it in my house,'
someone says. 'Not knowing where it's come from.'
As if objects soak up instability

like nicotine. If so, not only so –
for writhing up the staircase in Crichton Hall
are oak leaves, carved not by craftsmen from Antwerp,
but by men traipsing over winter fields
from Dalton using a water pipe as guide.
Run your hands over the leaves and you'll feel

their approval for their new asylum.
Though of the mad, little could be salvaged –
not one knitted pullover, not one apron –
for these craftsmen, the trade in lunacy
was a godsend. The melancholy we mourn
they transformed into bread, milk, sunlight.

New Poems

St Andrews

I am sitting in Pitigliano –
that human doocot, perched

on a spur of Tuscan rock –
thinking about St Andrews.

It's not so hard. February
in Tuscany's not how the pictures

play in your mind. I've seen
the charm of small-town piazzas

drabbed by a relentless
northern rain and otherwise

delightful alleys so grey and cold
you'd think them splashed with salt.

But, this evening, the day turned
and from the valley of the Meleta

Pitigliano appeared to float
on its honeyed rock against

a properly azure sky.
In memory, once again, I saw

how St Andrews would likewise
stoke up all the clarity

an East-coast day could offer,
till the town, miraculously, rose

on a bed of its very own golden
Tuscan light. Thus it floated

above Fife's soft landscape –
above cornfields, turnip drills and sea.

At such times, within the warmth
of its evening walls, I'd hear

the ruined campanile ring out,
soundlessly.

Stone Relief: Pitigliano

On a long rectangle
of volcanic stone
on the street-side wall

of the twelfth century
Church of San Rocco,
there's a carving in low

relief, easily missed.
It shows a nobleman,
whose beard's as neat

as an inverted candelabra,
with arms outstretched
and his hands, their tips

segmented like fruit,
held up to the wrists
in the fearsome teeth

of two winged dragons.
The symbolism of this
static drama, we're told,

'refers to the superiority
of spiritual strength
over brute force'.

With peach-stone eyes,
cast in the shadows
of his brows,

the face could be
described charitably
as 'thoughtful'. *Centred*,

we might now say.
Certainly, the man's keen
to conserve energy

to give nothing away.
For this is a stand off
if ever there were one.

Nine centuries later,
the Chinese-lantern-
jawed dragons show

no sign of loosening
their grip any time soon;
while he is still waiting –

without an eyelid's
flicker – for history
to prove his case.

Oven

In the crypt-like spaces
of Pitigliano's

subterranean ghetto,
the Jews enacted

their ancient rituals,
by which I mean

they – like the Etruscans
long before them –

lived their lives. In one,
the deep matzo oven

(last used in '39)
forms a double darkness.

In this windless place,
ash lasts. I rub

between forefinger
and thumb a pinch of it –

so soft and fine,
it leaves no mark.

Walnut Gatherers

Saepinum, Molise, Italy

Three men moving with purpose
and thought below the broad skirts
      of two walnut trees – at times
      in their shadows, at others

out on the ancient silvery stones
of Saepinum itself. They keep
      a proper distance from each other –
      there's ample for each

wherever they are –
though now and again,
      for none of the three is a young man,
      one briefly stands and sways

his back this way and that
before he dips again to the task.
      Per il dolce, I am told
      with a smile. The windfalls they want

have already slipped
their black jackets and hardened
      in the September sun
      to a semblance of wood. I take my foot

to one on a stone slab. It turns
to crumbs and shards. But for the second,
      my weight is perfect: the nut,
      all its foetal lines intact,

lifts out like a gift. The three men
drift away when their bags are full,
      leaning into the fading light
      to balance the knuckled weight.

They pass an arid fountain
inscribed by he who would be remembered
    for services once rendered
    this ruined provincial town.

Per il dolce. How right on such a day
to make time for sweetness: to mark presence,
    sunlight, silence, with the rhythmic
    click of walnut on walnut.

Spanish Shaving

As light dims, I take my shaver outside
to trim my holiday beard. The grey drifts
down to tinder-dry grasses; the small blades
chirr like insects as my blind hand sifts

through the stubble. That's when my wife appears
and sees at once something else we can share.
In tending each wanton bristle, she blanks
out all but the job at hand. A car roars

through the vineyards; a dog barks. The leaves
rattle in the almost breeze, while I lean
forward like an old man in surrender.
There was stubble behind his blue jaw-line

my father always missed. His late kisses
exposed it when, trusting in her answer,
he tipped his face towards my mother. His mask
briefly hovers in the warm evening air.

Between my face and it, my wife's sweet breath
travels the blind trajectory of love.

Choked

When the salt-and-pepper beef
stuck in my throat, I swallowed –
a couple of those vigorous movements
I'd seen cormorants do. Nothing. It felt
like a small fist had lodged there.

I finished my water,
sensing it sluicing down the sides
of the obdurate beef, then reached
for my opposite's lager. By now
my eyes were watering. I'd risen

a little from my chair. I pointed
to my throat. '*Choke-ing.*' Two syllables
it took my whole torso to make. One
of my companions slapped me on the back
to no effect. One vigorously embraced me.

But while my body panicked
a cooler self observed: So this is
the way it's to be. We can rarely
choose the style, but who'd have guessed
this? Now. Slumped over a table

in the Chinese Dragon
with my Friday football crowd
disappearing in a haze. Of course
we're not there yet. Still to come: the chopstick
thrust down the throat; the knife

ventilating the windpipe. Then
before the final convulsion, please,
a moment of calm to consider
the fish tank, the elegant movements
that will outlast me; to brave a smile

at those who stand over me –
those at tables I'll never now meet
but who acknowledge one of their own
is leaving: in such circumstances
each of us recognises a loss.

And then close to the end, I see you
rushing to me as you did that night
your dress caught fire from one
of the hearthside candles I'd always
cautioned you against. The flames

were already licking up your back
as they powered you towards me,
a look of horror or lust in your face.
A choking man, the Chinese (might) say,
will soon as not turn to water.

So as you settle on your man
like a fiery bird, let him, one last time,
douse your love with the last of his liquid breath
and let the light ashes of your dress
fall about us both like confetti.

The Worst Thing

We're lying one afternoon,
the children elsewhere, too tired to read,
talk almost beyond us. We begin
to play-pretend at being smokers. Whose hand
first lifts to their mouth? Whose first thought's
to give contentment a shape? Whatever,
it seems it's a secret craving, waiting to be met.
We inhale greedily,
hold our hands limply beyond our bedsides –
till we realise neither one of us is lit. The first
play-cigarettes crumble into ghosts of ghosts.
I tap the foot of my fist.
Two ciggies pop up.
I light them with my spare thumb
and we fall back into who we once were,
tracing ancient crop circles through the air.
An ashtray rests between our thighs.
Lethargy's in our veins –
the sexual drug mimicked
by exhaustion. You flick ash from the cover,
leaving a pencil-smear.
I take a final pull with a half-shut eye.
We stub out our butts. Losing no time
I flick out another, light it and pass it over to you.
'Oh yes,' you say, '*that* one.'
I could wonder who gave you this pleasure –
I having given up ten years before we met.
But the indrawn air's so calming, the sharing so sweet.
In my parents' wedding photo
my father cupped a cigarette behind his coat-tails;
the smoke gone with the breeze. Years later
I found a photo of our mother
lighting a cigarette from his. They were in a café
leaning towards each other; she breaking up
with laughter. I can hear him saying

to the holiday smoker:
'Michty me, Agnes, you've got to suck!'
'So you were happy?' I'd asked,
surprised by the urgency of the question.
'Oh yes, we were happy.'
Now you and I, drawing deeply on the last
cigarettes of the short afternoon,
imagine for a moment the worst things
our children, back early, could barge into our bedroom
and find us doing. Almost
top of the list comes playing at smoking
like small children used to do. My fish mouth
sends out smoke rings like I never could before.
You're wreathed in a gauze of smoke
like a forties starlet. Daft.
But I'd like to put on record for them
that, though their parents never smoked
together properly, there was an afternoon
in late summer, when they lay in bed
and were almost immediately
post-coitally happy, watching sunbeams
coalesce into smoke – white, rich and thick –
sharing with each other one more
tiny part of their histories.

Baleen

Lac Salagou, Languedoc

I

There's a particular light
      in Galloway I associate
with summer evenings, the sun
      slanting from a clear sky

the green hills lit from within.
      It's a common quality
in Dutch landscape art, grace
      blessing the mercantile world.

It shares something
      of the harsh light caught
by Winslow Homer, where the earth-lit
      face with humility

the threat of a coming storm.
      The light by the shore
of Lac Salagou this afternoon
      is none of these –

though what it shares
      with them is the clarity
of each object which falls
      within its gaze. So fierce

a light, there's little to contrast
      with it. Little shadow,
little break in the perfect blue sky.
      At lakeside,

in the scattered shadows
      of tall rushes, I look along
the gentle swells that hold each
      small creek and see the forms –

heads, torsos, limbs –
    of swimmers rise and fall
from the red geometry
    that is the region's earth.

The light gives me
    at a distance a group
of three – two teenage girls
    and a small boy. I pick out

the slick of the skin
    their youth holds so tightly to them
and the gentle swellings
    of adolescence: the need

to be aware of one's self
    in the most simple stance.
Clarity's everywhere,
    favouring nothing:

the vine, the fig-tree, the village
    shining in its cleft of rock –
the Hudson River School
    come to Lac Salagou.

But while these painters
    in their ecstasy
led your eye to light,
    it was through the ministry

of a traveller on a cliff-edge
    or river bend you were invited
to interpret the sight.
    The figures in this landscape

live in a democracy of light
    and light wherever it falls
is a servant of time.
    Here –

in the Theatre of the Dunes –
    each is separate, sealed,
in the possible meanings
    of his diminishing world.

II

I have a recurring dream
    of loneliness so sharp
it shakes me from my sleep.
    Often I've thought its cause

lay in some disappointment
    from my past – scorned love
imprinting years of forlornness
    on my heart. Now I wonder

whether my dream lies
    at a lakeside where I
and others go, so far from what we know
    it's impossible to get home again.

It's the loneliness there
    that'll break you. That I know.
Perhaps at their cores others have
    what's indestructible, something

they can touch like a stone.
    Perhaps it has a name.
For me there's this emptiness
    I don't know if I should fill –

it could be where I'm sitting now.
    The light that coats everything
at Lac Salagou, the veil of light
    the Dutch masters laid

over the curve of an egg,
    of course I've seen before.

The room my mother died in
        was bathed in much the same

unforgiving light. Each one
        of her crisp grey hairs, the eyes
trembling in their sockets,
        as she rose for each

jagged breath above her
        and almost out of reach.
But nothing of her was favoured
        over the cold struts

of the bedstead, the apparatus
        by her side, the clear cup
of the oxygen mask which kept
        her face from us till the end.

The colour of the whalebone
        that filters their tiny food,
that once made whips,
        spokes, combs and stays:

I saw something of it
        in her eyes and at the corners
of her lips and something like it –
        if I could only name it –

but thinner, characterised
        the hue of her tired skin.
As if her end would be marked
        with the colour of the world

she was born to – the ruched
        resins of Edwardian Britain.
(She bucks for breath; the whale dives.
        Again I chase the word.)

There was amber there too.
     The amber found in fat pulses
of bladderwrack or the thoughtlessness
     of sheep's eyes – pupils fixed

like insects, trapped, unseeing.
     She could go on like this
for hours, the nurse said. We looked at her,
     ungainly, exhausted, like someone

at the end of a race, yet each breath
     so surely following the other
and neither of us – daughter
     or son – willing to leave her.

But for whatever reason
     it's hard here to fathom,
we took to the bleak canteen
     and so she died alone.

I'm told it happens.
     The mirroring of a mother
seeing her children settled
     before she herself turns in.

Still, in the glare of that room,
     this seemed the greatest loneliness
and I only hope she was not aware –
     they promised not –

of how light held the seats
     beside her and did not dissemble
at the last. The precise coordinates
     of the dying breath of my mother

and my immediate next
     she took with her to the grave.
I put myself into that room
     but know I'll never nail the colour

or the taste. All I'll find
     is loneliness arching its back
on a hospital bed. I'm lying
     this afternoon at the lakeside.

Beside me, the sun curves
     round my son's right shoulder.
I reach for him there as you would
     for the warm taut skin of a pear

and turn his face from his own shadow.

Selkie

It was around the first time I recall
seal culls had featured on the evening news.
After tea, from deep in our couch, we'd watched
giant figures, padded like hockey stars

take their clubs onto the ice. The seal cubs'
mothers, at a distance, tipped back their heads –
their cries were almost human. The men dragged
the pelts, writing their blood into the snow.

Mum looked at the sealskin gloves where they lay,
still on their Christmas paper, in the sheen
of the tree lights, and in spite of our dad's
'Aye, they'll keep you warm, Agnes' glow, she knew

these gloves would never leave the house again
while she lived. Wary of the risk, she said,
'Someone might hack my hands off at the wrists.'
For hadn't she seen in the same news item,

as well as the calm killers, the close-ups
of the cull protesters too, their red eyes
fiery for justice? But at the least,
she acknowledged, Dad hadn't short-changed her –

misguidedly perhaps, he'd bought her the best.
She pulled them on and held them before her,
smiling, for my father. Her fingers were still,
the gloves clumsy, out of their element.

Each was a small pelt in itself; silver
and precious as it caught and shed the light.
They bore a glint of underwater ice
from that other world around their edges.

*

I never saw her wear the gloves again,
but from time to time, if visitors called,
she'd take them from the drawer they lived in –
buried beneath scarves, stoles and innocent

wearable gloves – like a secret to be shared.
They'd sit then on her lap and she'd stroke them
in the way that fisherwomen would care,
in selkie stories, for a baby seal

they'd saved from the cruel workaday world,
lifting it from the darkness when they could
and feeding it with snatches of sunlight.
At the end of such stories, it's understood

the grown seal finds its way home to the sea
and may even take the woman with it.
No longer human now like you or me,
she'll live on beneath the foam; though at times

you may glimpse a familiar old grey head
bobbing in the water and think you see,
from far out, a glistening fin wave –
before the seal dives back into the grave.

The Key

'In the Faroe Islands there is a proverb –
"She could no more hold herself back
than the seal wife could when she found her skin."'
         from *The People of the Sea*, David Thompson

When he was lying there in his pomp,
his face open as a book thrown aside –
a comic tale, let's say, a fisherman
might tell at market for an extra drink –

she smiled on him and filched the key
from his waistcoat pocket. She had it
copied that afternoon, returned, unnoticed,
by night. Though he could never put

a date on it, he took it from such a time
their true marriage began. For, one afternoon,
out of curiosity, in the same way
one might idle in the cove again

where one had first gone to ground
with a lover, he unlocked the wooden kist.
The skin lay there still, not tightly scrolled
as he had left it, but loosely bundled

as if she had let it fall, folding
softly in on itself, as he'd seen her
cast off clothes. (Nakedness had never
bothered her.) He held it to his face

and drew in again the first sharp smell
she'd brought from the sea. And shadowing it,
her other smells; the prints of salt and sea-pinks
she left like a spoor. He searched for signs

of struggle – on this and on other occasions –
the way the skin was twisted like a rope

of washing, or dust clung to it and a splinter
pierced the spot where she'd stamped it

into the wooden floor. The rime of her tears
was silver on the silver fur. (No, he'd never
been the easiest man to live with.) He rolled
the pelt up again and locked the kist.

Not a word was spoken on either side,
though in years to come, he'd hold up
the skin and see in it new indents she had made;
how it moulded the drop of her breasts

or followed the lip of her belly where their children
had grown. He'd stare through the blind holes
in the hood and he'd fail again and again
to see the world through her dark eyes.

But when times were hard between them,
he'd take the key to the kist and note the skin
folded in a new way, a sign – or so he took it –
that the element they were in was of their choosing.

Jenny (14) in July

flicks her hair from
the damp nape of her neck –
in Proteus's time,

'Daddy's bit'. She glows
like a coal as we trawl
through the arid

space of Olympia's
Temple of Zeus, at which
we have arrived

(as is our way)
bang in the middle
of this searing

July day. 'Can I
be honest with you guys?'
she says, peering

at the world through
bug-eyed Lady Di
shades, 'None of

this stuff means
a thing to me.' Funny
how you can tell.

The great columns
have collapsed like
giant clock wheels;

Zeus is not at all
what he was. Jenny
too has moved on –

to poetry. 'Dad,
can you write a poem
with all my friends in it?

Adele, Lauren,
Hannah, Lucy, Katie,
Abbey, Joanna, Connor

and Clark. But, oh no,
you'll probably write a poem
about old stones.'

Like this one,
my darling girl.
Like this one.

The Polish Faust

One year, festival-time, my son reminds me,
I took him to the Polish *Faust* – three hours for the money
and a five star review. Yet, in the cavernous theatre
at the Assembly Rooms, both wings were empty.

In a cinema, we would've scattered like sheep,
picnicked in twos or threes, yet here we huddled,
muttering 'excuse-mes' as we edged past others
as serious as ourselves. What, almost everyone

has asked since, had my thirteen-year-old son done
to deserve it? What lessons did his Presbyterian father
imagine were in store? 'Well, I wasn't bored,'
he confessed as the lights went up and even my heart

beat a little faster at the prospect of Danny Bhoy
an hour down the line. But now he tells me
he'd been terrified by a production, which held
all the virtues of the Polish avant-garde: faces

like bloodied candle wax, a babble of tongues
that mocked, whinnied or grieved. Mephisto
stalked the doomed Faust, ground him down
with remorseless *coups de théâtre*. My son

reminds me of what had slipped my mind –
that in the black cacophonous world
I'd abandoned him to brick it alone; managed
somehow to support my righteous head

and sold my soul to sleep. What lonely terrors
for him! What sweetness for me – to wake
in the corrupted world and to find my dear son
smiling bravely in the guttering light of doom.

St Nicholas

for Stewart Conn on his 70th

from the painting by Gerard David
in the National Gallery of Scotland

Up the hill from Fettes Row, I ponder
one of three Legends of St Nicholas,
wherein dressed as the Bishop of Myra
the saint gains revenge on the pitiless

by raising from the dead three chalky boys
salted down for meat in time of famine.
As his gloved hand makes the sign of the cross,
they rise like birds from their wooden coffin

lifting and closing their palms in prayer.
Nothing in his countenance appears amazed
that, with his touch, these bald nestlings should flare
into light. While, in the shadows, the dazed

murderers hear the bells begin to ring,
hunger for a saint's blessing, sealed with song.

The Annunciation

La Anunciación (c.1963–64) by Antonia Eiriz (1929–95),
Museo Nacional de Belles Artes, Havana

There's something of Charles Laughton
about the lumpen Virgin – a simple seamstress –
as she recoils in her chair, pinned
by a whey-faced light. She gasps for breath,
as neuralgic shockwaves pass through her.
And who can blame her, with only
a sewing machine between her
and the angel who comes at her
in a diagonal from top right
like something released from a trap,
so desperate has he been for this task.

One critic has commented on
'the ferocious savagery' of Eiriz's work
and truly, none of Dürer's Four Horsemen
is as terrifying as this skeletal ghoul.
We see the rack of his ribcage, his pelvic bone,
round as a wheel. There's nothing
behind his depthless square eyes;
though the gleeful horror
of his dark rectangular mouth
recalls the cage from which he's been sprung.
                                        His left arm –
a conjunction of serviceable bones –
appears fixed to the side of his head. It is from this
grim extension that the seamstress helplessly turns.

Yet he will deliver his message, eloquently
paraphrased thus: 'The good news?
There is no present from God, nor is God
a present. No mysticism nor life
breathes in this painting, only
the terrifying anguish which precedes the end.'

It is indeed an image of joyless force,
yet not without its majesty. The angel's wings,
the colour of ditch-water,
sweep out behind him like a cloak;
and above his fiery, almost molten brows,
a few brush strokes mark a crown.

Eiriz herself
fell from the firmament
sometime in the sixties, her work
attacked with such ferocious savagery
that she abandoned painting altogether.
Up close, you will find there's not a patch
of canvas that's without energy and interest.
That said, what regime would not fear one,
who, without a hint of madness, only with a
dolor activa, can look at the face of the world
with no illusion, hope or compromise
and then have the courage
to hold that image
for the time it takes
to exercise her virtuosity,
dipping her brush
again and again
into the darkness?

Shaman

for Pablo Armando Fernandez

Because he believes the ribcage
offers only temporary
shelter for the soul,
when he holds his hand
to a breastbone metaphors fly
from the spot. An angel
rises from one, great wings
thrashing the air, its host beneath it,
like an open grave. From another
an eagle rises into the air
and he shields his eyes
from its magnificence
and its claws. The mouth
of an orchid grows from another, red
as the blood which is its bond.
Into it, a hummingbird
smaller than a finger
dips its beak. Always
he says, when his fist
touches the breastbone – he never
has to strike – something
is released and even the smallest
birds with their bright eyes,
their articulate wings,
are of interest. Because
we are on his veranda
in late afternoon, the mango's
elegant leaves casting us
in early shadow, and because
I am full of his imagination, I see
birds with scarlet throats,
with wings of the most
intricate tapestry. But as,

his soft blue eyes on mine
all the while, he gently
touches my breast, I too feel
a stirring within me, some knuckle
unclench and wish to be known –
a curlew perhaps, a blackbird
or our combative garden robin.
And, as he knows that inside
each breast lies a bird
waiting to reveal its form –
though you may prefer
to see a flower, a fish or indeed
that angel – so he also knows
that which is most
frequently overlooked:
no matter the cold night
it must pass through, no matter
the silence in the garden, it remains
natural as breath for certain
very special birds
still to sing.

Etruscan

I hold up a hand to block out the town –
its fortress walls, its leaping aqueduct,
its airy campanile. I want to strip it

back to the rock again, to lower the eye
from the platform of light to those small arches
in the hillside which give darkness a shape.

I want to be close to the earth again,
to the forest floor, the river and the meadow,
with a people for whom Death's only

one more furnished room. Yesterday
a latter-day Etruscan led me, feeling
my way down, into the torch-lit caverns

of a *cantina* in whose tomblike spaces
she'd improvised a home. In an alcove
stood the gleaming sarcophagus of her bath.

(In Death, she'll hover over it, drawing back
the veil of her hair, a mirror in her hand.)
A deeper cavern glowed with the stripped

white fact of her bed. To both spaces
the shades lent their own erotic charge.
She'd wintered there, tending the green shoots

of herself while, up above, the gentlest
falling snow filled the fissures of the town,
and froze in its shadows. But now a cane man

stands in our piazza ready to burn
and I'm stumbling up beside a waterfall
already fringed with the first crocuses

and dog violets of spring. I make for
an excavated gloom and when I reach it
the low sun greases its threshold of nettles,

its thatch of brambles, and lays a path clear
across its dirt floor to fire the lichen
with an iridescent, coppery green.

I trace the walls of chisel marks. Each stroke,
the movement of an arm, unruffles stone.
'I think we've many lives in us,' she'd said

in the stony hollows she'd made her home.
'I want in one of mine to be that child again –
the one whose natural instinct's

to be drawn to the darkness of the cave;
and then to follow it, ever further, fearlessly
testing its contours, even when the light gives out.'

Notes

Rough Seas

The river mentioned in several of the poems in *Rough Seas* is the River Nith which runs through Dumfries.

The Moth Trap

'St Medan'
Kirkmaiden is a chapel on the Wigtown coast, dedicated to the Irish saint, Medan. There is a well on the foreshore, which was believed to possess miraculous curative powers for the blind.

Red Letter Day

The poems which open *Red Letter Day* concern a trip to the Dominican Republic and to Peru, Bolivia and Brazil in 1989. The later ones were written while I was holder of the Scottish Canadian Fellowship, based at the University of Alberta in Edmonton in 1991–92.

Sparks!

This collection was a poetic correspondence between myself and Diana Hendry. For two years we set each other poetic challenges. *Sparks!* (Mariscat, 2005) contains the poems, the sparks themselves and our responses to each task. 'Dear Alice' appeared again in the title which bears its name

Landscapes and Legacies

'Pilgrim'
The White Loch of Myrton is on the pilgrim route to Whithorn. It is said Robert the Bruce visited it, in the belief its waters cured leprosy.

The first lines of sections 14, 15, 16 and 17 of 'Landscapes' come from the following poems by Paul Reverdy: 'Son de Cloche', 'Secret', 'Et Maintenant' and 'Tard dans la Nuit'. 'Fionnghal' (section 14) is Gaelic for 'Flora'.

Transfusion

Transfusion draws on two trips I made to Africa. The first was soon after the Ali–Foreman fight in 1974; the second was in 1997. The coincidence of Mandela's inauguration, the twentieth anniversary of the Rumble in the Jungle and the birth of my daughter, Jenny Villette Lillian Pow, on St Patrick's Day 1994 was the inspiration behind *Transfusion*.

Dear Alice: Narratives of Madness

In 2000, I began to work for Glasgow University at the Crichton Campus in Dumfries, the site of one of the great nineteenth-century asylums. The poems in *Dear Alice: Narratives of Madness* are rooted in this experience.

'The Wolf Man at Crichton Hall, 1914'
Freud wrote the bulk of *From the History of an Infantile Neurosis*, in which the case of the Wolf Man is discussed, in autumn 1914, although it wasn't published until 1918.

'Freud at the Crichton'
Kraft-Ebbing was a sexologist in Vienna at the turn of the nineteenth century. He wrote extensively about sexual deviance.

'Grass'
Angus McPhee was a patient at Craig Dunain Asylum from the 1970s until the 1990s. He made clothes and shoes and many other objects from grass. Thank you to Joyce Laing for her analysis of McPhee's work in *Inner Necessity* (ed., Pat Fisher; 1996).